LATIN GRILLING

LATIN GRILLING

RECIPES TO SHARE, from **PATAGONIAN ASADO** to **YUCATECAN BARBECUE** and MORE

LOURDES CASTRO
PHOTOGRAPHY BY TARA DONNE

TEN SPEED PRESS
Berkeley

CONTENTS

INTRODUCTION

I'm a true Latin girl. I love to cook. I love to feed family and friends. And I love to spend hours lingering over a table with them while enjoying fabulous drinks and delicious food. My menus need to be diverse, the food abundant, and the flavors bright and vibrant. Oh, and one more thing: I want to feel as if I'm a guest at my own party.

That last part is a bit tricky, but after many years of trial and error I have figured out a way to make lots of delicious food and not feel as if I'm running a restaurant out of my house. More on that technique later—first let's talk about the food and the grill.

I love the taste of food that has been cooked with fire. The intense heat of the flames chars the food, deepening its flavor and enhancing its texture. Equally, I love how grilling draws a crowd and excites your guests. It must be the primal, communal aspect of cooking over flames that brings people together.

When I was growing up in Miami, I spent many weekends with my family grilling in our backyard. In line with our background, the foods and flavors were traditionally Cuban, while the grilling style and equipment varied according to the mood of the "grill master." I recall seeing everything from large sophisticated gas grills to small charcoal kettle ones. However, it wasn't all so arbitrary. Certain holidays, like Christmas Eve, called for the specific and ceremonial method of cooking a whole pig low and slow with charcoal. And on

school nights the gas grill was used for a quick flip of fresh fish over intense flames. Regardless of what was grilled or how it was made, the meal always seemed special.

As I got older and began traveling through Latin America, I saw firsthand how common cooking over fire, or grilling, was. I recall a visit to Argentina where I was lucky enough to be invited to a friend's home in the outskirts of Buenos Aires for a true, day-long Argentine *asado* (cookout). I've also experienced the freshest grilled fish prepared on a small charcoal kettle right on a beach in Ecuador, and had the best char-grilled pork tacos served out of a parked truck in Puerto Vallarta, Mexico. Each experience was different in its food and flavor, but the communal aspect was the same.

This brings me to an important note. Despite common threads, like grilling, all Latin food is not created equal. Latin America is a huge region made up of many countries, each with its own culinary history and characteristic flavors. Unfortunately, Latin fare tends to get muddled into one underwhelming cuisine. Just ask a Peruvian what he had for dinner and I guarantee you his answer will be very different than a Brazilian's. Yes, similarities do exist, but it's their differences—like the prominent use of cumin in one country and the focus on fiery chiles in another—that make the cuisines and their flavors so enticing.

In order to bring focus to the diversity and uniqueness of the cuisines of Latin America, I have organized this book by region, creating menus that provide a taste of some of the most popular foods of several countries. At the start of each chapter, I will set you up with quick pointers on what makes up the spirit of each cuisine and acquaint you with some of its key ingredients. My hope is that this will help you make out the subtle differences between the foods of Chile and Argentina, as well as the marked differences between those of Mexico and Brazil.

This book not only offers both grilling tips and lessons on Latin flavors, it also instructs you on how to pull off a full menu, from drinks to dessert, and still find time to enjoy yourself. To guarantee that you will be a guest at your own party, I've created a detailed "Game Plan" for each menu that outlines, step by step, what needs to be done in order to execute the menu successfully. You will see a chronological list of tasks as well as instructions on storage. Because, let's face it: most of us do not have a walk-in refrigerator where we can store trays of food!

One last thing: feel free to mix and match. Cook through the book, pick your favorites, and create your own menu. The only thing that matters is that the food is delicious and you are having a good time!

GUIDE TO GRILLING

Cooking with fire requires instinct. Understanding how to adjust the grill temperature and figuring out the precise time to remove meat from the grill will determine whether a steak turns out beautifully charred and succulent or dried and burnt. I'm not going to gloss over the fact that it takes trial and error to truly internalize many of the nuances involved with grilling. But ultimately, its not rocket science and once you're past the initial learning curve you'll find that much of the process becomes second nature. To get you started (or give you a refresher) I here are my top ten tips to get you successfully cooking over live fire in no time. Now, let's get grilling!

MY TOP TEN GRILLING TIPS

I. KNOW YOUR GRILL

All grills are not created equal. Each grill has its own nuances—how hot it gets, the hot spots, its tendency to flare. For this reason, you should treat all grilling recipes simply as guides. Once you're comfortable with your grill's capabilities, you will be able to better gauge cooking times and to use the lid to increase or decrease the intensity of the heat.

2. ALWAYS PREHEAT YOUR GAS GRILL

I always preheat my gas grill at least 15 minutes before I am ready to grill. I start by turning on the burners to their highest setting and allowing the grates to get very hot. Regardless of the temperature I will eventually cook my food at, this allows for an intense sear at the beginning of the grilling process. After the initial sear, I adjust my grill temperature as required.

3. INVEST IN A GOOD INSTANT-READ THERMOMETER

Forget about prodding the meat with your finger or just blindly guessing if your meat is properly cooked. Even professional chefs use thermometers to accurately measure the internal temperature of meats. Get yourself a good instant-read thermometer with a long, heat-resistant handle. I prefer those with thin probes that make small incisions in the meat, and I tend to stay away from those with thick two-prong forks.

4. EQUIP YOURSELF WITH THE PROPER TOOLS

There are four specific tools I find indispensable: long-handled tongs, a long-handled spatula, a long-handled basting brush, and a tight-fitting heat-resistant glove. The first three are pretty common, since they make up most sets of barbecue tools; just make sure the ones you use are heat resistant. The tight glove is a discovery I made after I got tired of singeing my hand when reaching the back of the

> Throughout the book I begin recipes by letting you know how high to set your grill along with the temperature that typically corresponds to that setting. For example, the citrus and oregano split chicken on the bone from the Mexican Frontera chapter starts on high (550°F) and finishes cooking at medium-high (450°F). Because temperature settings can differ significantly from grill to grill, you will need to treat these numbers as general indicators and understand that cooking times will vary accordingly.

grill—I figured there had to be a better way. I had always shied away from bulky grilling mitts, which were clumsy and never allowed me to feel as if I had a good grip on things. Then one day I found a pair of tight-fitting pit mitts that protected me from the heat of the flames but still allowed a good grip. Now I never grill without them.

5. ALWAYS OIL YOUR GRATES

Regardless of what you are grilling, it is always a good idea to properly oil your grates beforehand. Wait until your grill is hot and you are ready to place your food on the grate. I prefer using plain vegetable oil, slathering it onto the grates with a paper towel that I hold with long-handled tongs. This allows me to cover the entire grill area without burning myself.

6. DEAL WITH FLARE-UPS PROPERLY

Flare-ups, which are caused by oil or excess fat dripping into the fire, are not always bad, since they can result in a nice char. However, if uncontrolled they can result in scorched food. Here are some tips for preventing and dealing with flare-ups:

* If you're working with an oil-based marinade, allow as much marinade as possible to drip off the meat before placing it on the grill.
* If possible, create a low-heat zone on your grill as a safe haven to move your food to when flare-ups occur.
* If you don't have enough space for a low-heat zone, pile up pieces of food in a corner where the flare-up is not occurring while you wait for the flare-up to die down.
* You don't want to extinguish the flames with water for the same reason you don't pour water on a kitchen grease fire: the flames will just get bigger.

7. SOAK WOODEN SKEWERS AND PLANKS SUFFICIENTLY

I say this from experience: make sure to soak your wooden skewers for at least 20 minutes and your wooden planks for at least 2 hours. Anything short of that will result in the wood charring and possibly igniting.

I place skewers in a pitcher of water and, if they're not completely submerged, I flip them after twenty minutes to soak the rest. To soak wooden planks, I find it easiest to place them in a rectangular baking dish filled with water and set a heavy pot over the planks to keep them submerged.

8. HAVE A PLAN BEFORE YOU BEGIN

Understanding cooking times—and how well foods will hold after they come off the grill—is essential to successfully pulling off a grilling menu. If your menu is varied, begin by grilling the items that can be eaten at room temperature. Keep in mind that meat needs to rest for at least 5 minutes before you serve or slice it; this resting time can often be used to quickly grill some other items.

When grilling various cuts of meat, start with those that take the longest, adding the others along the way. This will ensure that they finish cooking at approximately the same time.

The same premise holds true when you're cooking the same cut of meat to various levels of doneness. Start with the pieces you want to end up well done, adding the medium well, medium, and so forth so that they all get done at about the same time.

9. TALK A WALK (OR HAVE A DRINK)

One of the biggest mistakes made by grillers is that they put food on the grill and immediately begin to mess with it. My rule is to put it down and walk away. In order for meat or vegetables to get a nice char, they need to spend some alone time with the heat. How long you leave the food alone depends on the food, but at least 5 minutes is a good start. Just enough time to get something cold to drink!

DONENESS TIPS

Remember that meats continue cooking after you have removed them from the grill. As a rule of thumb, remove large, thick cuts of meat when they hit 10 degrees below your desired temperature. Small, thin cuts should be removed about 5 degrees before they reach their mark. The following chart provides doneness guidelines for beef, veal, lamb, and pork.

Doneness	Description	Final Internal Temperature
Rare	Center is bright red; pinkish exterior	120–125°F
Medium rare	Center is very pink, slightly brown exterior	130–135°F
Medium	Pale pink center, brown exterior	140–145°F
Medium well	No pink in center	150–155°F
Well done	Brown throughout	160°F

Keep in mind:
- Pork should be cooked to medium or medium well.
- All types of sausage should be cooked to 160°F.
- Poultry should be cooked to 165°F.
- Fish should be cooked to desired doneness.

10. ALWAYS CLEAN YOUR GRILL PROPERLY AFTER EACH USE

This might sound obvious, but I can't tell you how many grills I have seen with bits of food caked onto their grates. Food sticks to dirty grates, and by not cleaning your grill, you are sabotaging yourself. Simply get yourself a cleaning brush with stiff bristles and, when you are done grilling, crank up the heat to the highest setting, wait for 5 minutes, and brush off any remaining food or oil residue from the grates.

GRILLING WITH GAS

Grills come in all shapes and sizes and use a variety of fuel sources. Before you decide between a large or small grill, custom-built or off the rack, your first choice when selecting a grill is usually between grills that use gas, wood, or charcoal fuel. The ease and convenience of gas grills has made them the most popular type of grill used today, so I developed the recipes in this book with gas grills in mind. However, that doesn't necessarily mean that you have to sacrifice the smoky flavor imparted by a wood grill or the intense char from a charcoal grill. When time permits, I bring out my small kettle charcoal grill and use the same recipes, making simple adjustments in cooking times; I'll guide you through those adjustments in the next section. Luckily, the effect of grilling over wood can also be achieved on a gas grill with simple and handy alternatives that I'll go over in the following pages.

GRILLING WITH WOOD

Grilling with wood does more than simply cook your food; it infuses it with a rich smoky flavor. Wood smoke also imparts a deep tan hue to the food. I've found that with the exception of those with special outdoor wood-burning ovens, most backyard grillers never grill with wood. This is really a shame, since they are missing out on so much flavor. I must admit, I'm not one to start splitting wood to create a fire for a backyard cookout. But I do use easier alternatives, like wood chips and wooden planks. Give it a shot—I promise you won't be disappointed!

I tend to use hickory, apple, or cherrywood chips. Hickory gives food an intense smoky flavor, while the cherry and apple are a bit milder.

WOOD CHIPS

Convenient and easy to use, these very small pieces of irregularly shaped wood are great for adding a smoky flavor to grilled meats, fish, and vegetables.

In order to prevent the chips from burning, which will turn your food bitter, soak the chips well before using them. If your grill has a built-in smoker, or if you are using a grill-top smoker, follow the manufacturer's instructions. Otherwise create foil packets of chips for smoking, as described below.

FIRST, DETERMINE HOW MANY WOOD CHIPS ARE NEEDED. In order to achieve an even smoke, I create three small packets of soaked wood chips and place them at various spots under the grill grates. I use about a handful of wood chips per packet. Keep in mind these foil packets will produce smoke for about 30 minutes. If your food requires a longer cooking time, create extra packets and replace them every half hour or when your packets are smoked out.

SECOND, SOAK THE WOOD CHIPS. Place the wood chips in a bowl filled with water. Push them under the water a few times to help start the soaking process. Allow the chips to soak for 1 hour, then drain.

NEXT, PREPARE PACKETS OF CHIPS. Cut three pieces of heavy-duty aluminum foil, each about 12 inches long. (It's best to use heavy-duty foil for the packets; however, you can substitute two layers of regular foil.) Place a handful of the soaked wood chips in the center of each piece of foil and spread the chips out a bit. Fold the sides of the foil over the chips, creating a packet that is sealed tightly. Using the tip of a sharp knife, make small slits all over the top of each foil packet.

FINALLY, SMOKE THE CHIPS. Place the foil packets under the grill grates. If possible, place the packets so they will not be sitting directly under the food (for example, place them at the back of the grill). Turn the grill on to the highest setting, close the lid, and wait for the wood to begin to smoke. It should take 10 to 15 minutes, but will vary with your grill. You should see smoke escaping from the sides of the grill when it's ready. If using a charcoal grill, place the packets over the coals after they have turned a pale ashy color and have been arranged on the bottom grate. Cover the grill and wait for the wood to begin to smoke.

WOODEN GRILLING PLANKS

I love grilling fish on these thin wooden planks, because then I don't have to worry about my fish sticking to or falling in between the grates (and cleanup is a snap). The planks won't give you grill marks, but they will give you moist, smoky fish that takes on a deep tan color from the smoke.

Make sure you soak the planks (that is, submerge them completely in water) for at least 2 hours. I've learned the hard way that insufficiently soaked planks will quickly incinerate. The planks are disposable, so you can simply discard them after you are done using them.

WOOD AS A HEAT SOURCE

Wood adds color and smoky flavor to food. But what's the difference between grilling with wood and grilling with charcoal—why not just build a wood fire in a charcoal grill and cook the food that way?

Wood creates a good amount of smoke, which is something to consider if you are grilling in a crowded setting. When you're grilling with wood you also must wait a long time for the flames to settle and the embers to reach the proper intensity. The bottom line? Grilling over a wood fire works, but it requires time and space.

GRILLING WITH CHARCOAL

I have very fond memories of spending weekends at the beach grilling ocean-side over small portable charcoal grills. We didn't cook anything complicated—usually hamburgers and hot dogs— but I remember them being the best hamburgers and hot dogs I had ever eaten. I'm sure the food was good enough, but I don't doubt it was the ceremonial aspect of building and cooking over a beachside charcoal fire that tricked my taste buds into thinking they'd never encountered anything so delicious.

Charcoal grilling was much simpler back then. There weren't many options when it came to the charcoal, and almost all fires were started with lighter fluid. Today many more charcoal choices exist, but the desired end result of mouth-watering grilled food is still the same. However, before you can begin creating new charcoal-grilled memories, you have to understand your options.

BEFORE YOU START

WHAT DO YOU NEED? You'll need a charcoal grill, charcoal, a chimney starter (optional), newspaper or lighter cubes, and long matches or a gas lighter.

WHAT TYPE OF CHARCOAL SHOULD YOU USE? Charcoal is wood that has been burned to remove its water and resins, leaving behind pure fuel. Charcoal is prized for grilling because, compared to wood, it reaches a high temperature quickly with little smoke.

Today you have a choice in charcoal. The two main types are charcoal briquettes and lump charcoal. Briquettes are the dark, square pieces of charcoal most of us are familiar with, while lump charcoal looks like jagged, irregular pieces of coal. In order to get briquettes shaped into uniform squares, binders and fillers are mixed in with the burnt wood and the briquettes are compressed into its form. Below are my pluses and minuses for each type of charcoal.

Briquettes
+ Produce less smoke
+ Produce even heat for a long time
+ Burn slower, requiring less replenishing
+ Are great for quick-cooking foods
− The heat produced is less intense
− Some feel the binders and fillers interfere with the pure flavor of the charcoal

Lump
+ Produces intense heat
+ Produces a clean burn with no off flavors
− Burns quickly and must be replenished more often
− Provides more smoke than briquettes; not ideal for small or crowded spaces

If you cannot decide between the two, a third option is available. Pure hardwood briquettes, also known as natural charcoal, basically combine the best features of briquettes and lump charcoal.

Natural Charcoal
+ Made of wood and bound with natural starches for a cleaner burn than standard briquettes
+ Burns almost as hot as lump charcoal
+ Produces a long, even heat, like briquettes
− A bit more expensive than regular charcoal

PREPARING AND LIGHTING THE COALS

HOW MUCH CHARCOAL DO YOU NEED? A good rule of thumb is to use 1 pound of charcoal (about 30 briquettes) per pound of meat.

HOW SHOULD YOU LIGHT THE CHARCOAL? I find that the easiest and safest way to light a charcoal fire is with a chimney starter. To use it, remove the top grate from the grill, fill the chimney starter with coals, and place it on the bottom grill grate. Place crumpled newspaper under the starter and light with a gas lighter or long match. The fire will ignite the coals. Wait until most of the coals turn a pale gray ashy color, then pour them onto the bottom grate and, using a long metal fork or spatula, arrange them as desired (in a heap to one side for a hot side and a cool side, or in an even layer for a consistent heat level). Finish by putting the top grate back into place. Your charcoal fire is now ready to go.

GRILLING THE MEAT

HOW TO GRILL QUICK-COOKING CUTS Meats that cook in less than 30 minutes are considered quick cooking (boneless chicken breasts or cutlets, sausages, burgers, kebabs, chops, steaks, and so on). The best way to grill these cuts is over intense, even heat, which is achieved by evenly distributing the coals over the bottom grate.

HOW TO GRILL SLOWER-COOKING CUTS Tough or large cuts of meat such as ribs, brisket, and pork shoulder, which require more than 30 minutes to cook, should be seared over high heat, then cooked until done over moderately high heat. In order to do this, create two heat zones on your grill by piling most of the charcoal on one half of the bottom grate. This large pile will produce intense heat: place your meat on the grate directly over the pile to sear it. Then move the meat over to the other half of the grill grate—the cooler, or indirect heat side—to continue cooking. Now close the grill lid to trap the heat and allow your meat to finish cooking.

While charcoal delivers intense heat, it does burn down and may need to be replenished during the time that you're grilling. There are two cues for when to restock your charcoal, one visual and one by feel. If you see quite a bit of ash build up around your coals, chances are you'll need to add more charcoal. (Ash is a sign of combusted coal, but also mutes the heat of still-live coals.) But before adding more, place your hand 1 inch above the grill grate to gauge how much heat the coals are emitting. If you can hold your hand above the grate for 2 seconds you're cooking over high heat, 3 seconds is medium-high heat, 4 seconds is medium, and so on.

Most charcoal grills have a hinged top grate that lifts up to allow you to add more coals. When you've determined that it's time to do so, move your food off of the hinged area and use long-handled tongs to lift open the grate; place new coals over the burning coals (it will take a few minutes before the heat begins to intensify).

ONCE YOU'RE DONE

WHAT DO YOU DO WITH THE BURNT CHARCOAL AND ASHES WHEN YOU'RE DONE GRILLING? Wait for the charcoal to burn out completely, turn to ash, and cool down before you dispose of it.

RUBS, MARINADES & GLAZES

Throughout this book you will find all sorts of flavor combinations that add vibrancy and zest to your food through the use of herbs, spices, and condiments. Latin cuisine is known for its pop of flavor, so feel free to pick out one of the many rubs, marinades, or glazes found here and turn your simple weeknight grilled chicken breast into something exciting.

Clockwise, from top left: Chipotle Chile Rub, Chile Rub, and Coffee Rub

USING RUBS

Rubs are combinations of dry spices. They may or may not contain sugar.

* Rubs that contain brown sugar should be stored in the freezer to prevent the sugar from drying out and turning into hard clumps.
* Spice rubs should be applied about 5 minutes before you are ready to grill. The salt in the rub may dry out your meat if you leave it on longer.
* If your rub does not contain salt, make sure to season your food before applying the rub.
* Make sure your grill grates are oiled before placing rub-crusted food on them.

USING MARINADES

Marinades are combinations of wet and dry ingredients that may include fresh herbs, spices, vinegar, wine, and/or citrus juices. They may or may not contain oil.

* Be alert, as oil-based marinades can cause flare-ups on the grill.

- Fish should not be left in highly acidic marinades for more than 20 minutes.
- To ensure evenly marinated meat, place your meat and marinade in a resealable plastic bag and press out as much air as you can before sealing.

USING GLAZES

Glazes are combinations of wet and dry ingredients, either sweet or savory, that are brushed onto food to give it a glossy appearance. Most grilling glazes have some sort of sugary ingredient, such as honey or fruit pulp, that acts as a caramelizing agent.

- Lower your heat a bit when adding glazes as the sugars they contain can easily burn and turn bitter.
- Adding a pinch of cayenne to a glaze helps balance the sweetness and gives it a subtle kick.

Clockwise,
from top center:
Ancho Chile Paste,
Citrus Oregano Marinade,
Chimichurri, Achiote Marinade,
Citrus Garlic Marinade, Soy &
Chile Marinade

Rubs	Marinades		Glazes
Chipotle Chile Rub (page 27) *Mexican Frontera Cookout*	Citrus Oregano Marinade (page 29) *Mexican Frontera Cookout*	Citrus Garlic Marinade (page 77) *Cuban Cookout*	Honey Lime Glaze (page 27) *Mexican Frontera Cookout*
Chile Rub (page 46) *Yucatecan Barbecue*	Ancho Chile Paste (page 24) *Mexican Frontera Cookout*	Soy & Chile Marinade (page 114) *The Peruvian Grill*	Honey Apple Cider Glaze (page 50) *Yucatecan Barbecue*
Coffee Rub (page 62) *Nicaraguan Ranch Roast*	Achiote Marinade (page 47) *Yucatecan Barbecue*	Fresh Parsley Sauce/ Chimichurri (page 152) *The Argentine Grill*	Coconut Lime Glaze (page 175) *Brazilian Rodizio*
Sauces			
Guacamole (page 22) *Mexican Frontera Cookout*	Fiery Tomato Salsa (page 53) *Yucatecan Barbecue*	Fresh Tomato Salsa (page 99) *Northern Andean Barbecue*	Charred Corn Salsa (page 160) *Chilean Seafood Cookout*
Charred Tomatillo Sauce (page 32) *Mexican Frontera Cookout*	Chunky Fresh Tomato Sauce/ Pico de Gallo (page 63) *Nicaraguan Ranch Roast*	Spicy Yellow Chile Sauce (page 116) *The Peruvian Grill*	Chilean Hot Pepper Salsa/ Salsa Pebre (page 166) *Chilean Seafood Cookout*
Chipotle Crema (page 33) *Mexican Frontera Cookout*	Garlicky Cuban Mojo (page 77) *Cuban Cookout*	Huancaina Sauce (page 119) *The Peruvian Grill*	Hot Pepper & Lime Sauce (page 180) *Brazilian Rodizio*
Pineapple Salsa (page 24) *Mexican Frontera Cookout*	Mango Salsa (page 81) *Cuban Cookout*	Fresh Parsley Sauce/ Chimichurri (page 152) *Nicaraguan Ranch Roast*	Smoked Paprika Oil (page 179) *Brazilian Rodizio*
Crema (page 30) *Mexican Frontera Cookout*	Tangy Avocado Sauce/Salsa Guasca (page 100) *Northern Andean Barbecue*		

Mexican Frontera Cookout

Drinks

Margarita {18}

Starters

Grilled Quesadillas with Charred
Poblano & Jalapeño Chiles /
Quesadillas de Rajas {19}

Two Guacamoles: Traditional
& Chipotle {22}

Main Courses

Chile-Marinated Pork Tacos with
Pineapple Salsa / *Tacos al Pastor* {24}

Chipotle-Rubbed Skirt Steak Tacos /
Tacos al Carbon con Chipotle {27}

Citrus- & Oregano-Marinated
Split Chicken / *Pollo Entero Adobado
con Jugo Citrico y Oregano* {29}

Condiments & Sides

Crema {30}

Charred Green Onions {31}

Charred Tomatillo Sauce {32}

Grilled Corn on the Cob with
Chipotle Crema & Queso Fresco /
Elote a la Parilla {33}

Fresh Radish & Cucumber Salad {36}

Beer-Stewed Beans with Chiles /
Frijoles Borrachos {37}

Dessert

Mexican Chocolate Cupcakes
with Cajeta Buttercream {38}

The northern Mexican frontera, or border, is home to a very distinct style of cooking. The area is landlocked, so fish and shellfish are seldom seen; beef, chicken, and pork are major proteins, as are dried beans. The prominence of beans comes from the large Aztec influence, which still exists today. This important indigenous civilization is also responsible for the cuisine's emphasis on corn and corn-based foods (think grilled sweet corn, tortillas, tamales, and so on) as the corn (maize) crop was central to the Aztec traditions. Fiery chiles, both fresh and dried, and especially chipotles, are essential to frontera cooking, as are intense spices such as cumin and dried oregano. Tomatoes, cilantro, and lime are also key ingredients.

{MENU GAME PLAN}

One day in advance:
- Bake the cupcakes (hold off on making the buttercream). Cover with plastic wrap. Storage: room temperature
- Soak the beans. Storage: room temperature

The night before:
- Cook the beans. Storage: refrigerator
- Marinate the pork. Storage: refrigerator
- Marinate the chicken. Storage: refrigerator
- Prepare the rub for the steak. Storage: freezer
- If making homemade crema, do it now. Storage: refrigerator
- Prepare the chipotle crema for the corn. Storage: refrigerator

On the morning of:
- Make the buttercream and pipe onto the cupcakes. Storage: room temperature
- Crumble the queso fresco. Storage: room temperature
- Prepare the charred tomatillo sauce. Storage: room temperature

- Roast and char the chiles for the quesadillas. Storage: room temperature
- Prepare the radish & cucumber salad. Storage: refrigerator
- Prepare the pineapple salsa for the pork tacos. Storage: room temperature

Two to three hours before:
- Prepare a pitcher of margaritas. Storage: refrigerator
- Bring the beans and the crema to room temperature.
- Soak the corn.
- Assemble the quesadillas and cover with a damp towel. Storage: room temperature
- Start the guacamole by mincing or grinding the aromatic vegetables. Do not add avocado yet. Storage: room temperature
- Wash and trim the green onions. Storage: room temperature
- Make the tortilla packets. Storage: room temperature

In the hour before (setup):
- Begin to reheat the beans.
- Set up the beverage bar with margarita pitcher, ice, and glasses.

- Bring out to table:
  Chips for guacamole
  Tomatillo sauce
  Crema
  Queso fresco
  Pineapple salsa

As your event unfolds:
- Serve margaritas.
- Finish the guacamole(s) by mashing in the avocado and seasoning.
- Grill the quesadillas.
- Serve the starters.
- Grill the chicken.
- Grill the corn in its husks.
- Grill the pork.
- Remove the husks and char the corn.
- Place the rub on the steak and grill.
- Oil, season, and grill the green onions.
- Heat the tortillas.
- Bring out the radish and cucumber salad.
- Bring out the beans.
- Serve the main courses and sides.
- Serve dessert.

MARGARITA

I don't know what it is about margaritas, but I find they immediately make everyone relaxed and happy. And whether you like yours frozen or on the rocks, with or without salt, this classic cocktail is a snap to make. I like to prepare a pitcher of margaritas a few hours in advance and keep it chilled so I'm ready for my guests as soon as they arrive (see Cooking Notes, below). **Makes 1 cocktail**

Salt for rimming the glass (optional)
Ice
1½ ounces tequila
1 ounce lime juice (from 1 to 2 limes)
½ ounce Cointreau

PREPARE THE GLASS If using, pour a handful of salt on a small dish. Use a damp napkin to wet the edges of the rim of a short rocks glass and invert it onto the dish to rim the glass with salt.

MIX THE COCKTAIL Fill the glass with ice and add the tequila, lime juice, and Cointreau. Stir well and serve.

COOKING NOTES

INGREDIENTS

Cointreau Cointreau is a premium brand of triple sec produced in France. It is an orange-flavored liqueur made from the dried peels of Seville oranges.

ADVANCE PREPARATION

The margarita recipe can easily be multiplied and mixed in a pitcher several hours in advance.

To make a pitcher for 8:
12 ounces tequila
8 ounces fresh lime juice
4 ounces Cointreau

Keep the pitcher refrigerated and pour the margaritas into salt-rimmed, ice-filled glasses when you are ready to serve.

FROZEN LIMEADE MARGARITA
Try this for an unexpected twist! **SERVES 6 TO 8**

Ice
6 ounces frozen limeade concentrate
6 ounces tequila
2 ounces Cointreau

Fill a blender all the way with ice. Add the frozen limeade concentrate, tequila, and Cointreau. Blend until smooth. Serve and enjoy!

GRILLED QUESADILLAS with Charred Poblano & Jalapeño Chiles {QUESADILLAS DE RAJAS}

Grilled quesadillas are fun, easy starters for any cookout. These ubiquitous Mexican snacks are as easy to assemble as they are to grill and will immediately whet your guests' appetites. I love the charred smokiness that roasted poblano chiles (*rajas*) provide, and my "hot-head" friends love the added jalapeños. If you are not a fan of the heat, substitute grilled or sautéed mushrooms , bell peppers, or green onions for the chiles. **Makes 6 quesadillas**

4 poblano chiles
6 jalapeño chiles
3 cups shredded Monterey Jack cheese
12 corn tortillas
Vegetable oil

Charred Tomatillo Sauce (page 32)
Crema, homemade (page 30) or store bought

ROAST THE CHILES Heat your grill to high (550°F) and close the lid. Wait at least 15 minutes before continuing.

Oil the grill grates with a vegetable oil–soaked paper towel held with a long pair of tongs.

Place the poblano and jalapeño chiles directly on the grill grates and allow them to char on all sides (you are looking for the skin to turn black). It should take about 3 minutes per side for a total of about 12 minutes. To help speed the process, close the grill lid. When the chiles are charred all over, seal them in a plastic bag and set aside for 5 minutes. This will trap steam, allowing the skins to separate from the flesh. If you are going to grill the quesadillas right away, keep the grill on high and close the lid.

{CONTINUED ON NEXT PAGE}

COOKING NOTES

INGREDIENTS

Poblano chiles These dark green chiles measure up to 5 inches in length and have an intensely fruity flavor with very mild heat. Roasted poblanos sliced into strips are referred to as *rajas*, a term that also applies to other roasted and sliced chiles.

Monterey Jack cheese Monterey Jack is a semihard cow's milk cheese that melts very well. It is the American cheese most similar to queso Oaxaca, which is a mozzarella-style cheese traditionally used in Mexico for quesadillas.

Crema Do not confuse this Mexican staple with sour cream. Mexican crema is saltier and has a thinner consistency despite its richer flavor. It serves as a neutralizer for the heat of chiles, making it a great option to have around for those who don't like their food too hot.

ADVANCE PREPARATION

The chiles can be roasted well in advance. The quesadillas can be preassembled and left at room temperature with a damp towel covering them so the corn tortillas do not dry out.

It is best to grill the quesadillas right before serving, as the cheese tends to turn gummy as it sits.

Remove the chiles from the bag, cut off the stems, and, if desired, remove the seeds (this will decrease the heat). Lightly scrape the charred skin off the chiles with the blade of your knife. Alternatively, if your skin is not sensitive to the hot chiles, you can remove the skin with your fingers. To preserve their smoky flavor, do not rinse the chiles under water; it's okay if some of the charred skin stays attached to the chile. Cut the chiles into long strips. Set aside.

ASSEMBLE THE QUESADILLAS Place a tortilla on your work surface and top with approximately ¼ cup of cheese. Lay about ⅙ of the roasted chile strips over the cheese and top with another ¼ cup of cheese and a second corn tortilla. Repeat with the remaining ingredients until you've formed 6 quesadillas.

GRILL THE QUESADILLAS If your grill is not heated, heat your grill to high (550°F) and close the lid. Wait at least 15 minutes before lowering the heat to medium-high and continuing.

Lightly brush one side of the quesadillas with vegetable oil and place them oiled side down on the grill. Cook for 4 to 5 minutes, or until the bottom tortilla develops grill marks and turns golden brown.

Lightly brush the tops of the quesadillas with a bit more vegetable oil and, being careful not to break them open, flip them over and cook for another 3 minutes.

SERVE Allow the quesadillas to cool for a few minutes before cutting in half or quarters. Serve with the charred tomatillo sauce and the crema.

TWO GUACAMOLES: TRADITIONAL & CHIPOTLE

I can't think of any food that brightens up a party more than guacamole—a staple at all Mexican parties. There never seems to be enough—and when you see how easy it is to make, you will be preparing buckets of it (you will never buy premade guacamole again). Here, I am giving you two variations: one is for traditionalists who like their guacamole made simply with a jalapeño, while the other adds an element of smokiness by incorporating a chipotle chile. Serves 10

TRADITIONAL GUACAMOLE

¼ white onion, coarsely chopped (about ¼ cup)
1 jalapeño chile, stemmed, seeded (optional), and chopped
½ cup lightly packed cilantro leaves and tender stems, plus a few sprigs for garnish
1 teaspoon kosher salt
3 Hass avocados
1 tablespoon lime juice (from ½ to 1 lime)

CREATE A PASTE WITH THE VEGETABLES Put the chopped onion in a mound in the center of your cutting board. Top it with the chopped jalapeño and then the cilantro. Sprinkle the salt over the vegetables. Using a sharp chef's knife, chop and crush the vegetables until they are very finely minced into a paste. The salt will cause some of the moisture to be drawn out from the vegetables, which will help to blend their flavors.

Transfer the vegetable paste to a medium bowl.

SCOOP OUT AND MASH THE AVOCADOS Cut the avocados in half lengthwise and remove the seeds. Using a spoon, scoop out all of the flesh and place it in the bowl with the vegetables.

A potato masher or tart tamper is a great tool for this next step. If you don't have either, a dinner fork will do just fine.

Mash the avocado until you achieve the consistency you want. The texture is entirely up to you.

Some people like their guacamole chunky, while others prefer it smooth. I like it somewhere in the middle, where I can see some chunks of avocado but most of it is well blended.

SEASON WITH LIME JUICE AND SERVE Add the lime juice to the guacamole and combine well. Taste for seasoning and adjust if needed.

Place the guacamole in a serving bowl and garnish with cilantro sprigs.

CHIPOTLE GUACAMOLE

¼ white onion, coarsely chopped (about ¼ cup)
1 canned chipotle chile, stemmed and chopped
½ cup lightly packed cilantro leaves and tender stems, plus a few sprigs for garnish
1 teaspoon kosher salt
3 Hass avocados
1 tablespoon lime juice (from ½ to 1 lime)

CREATE A PASTE WITH THE VEGETABLES Put the chopped onion in a mound in the center of your cutting board. Top it with the chopped chipotle chile and then the cilantro. Sprinkle the salt over the vegetables. Using a sharp chef's knife, chop and crush the vegetables until they are very finely minced into a paste. The salt will cause some of the moisture to be drawn out from the vegetables, which will help to blend their flavors. Transfer the vegetable paste to a medium bowl.

SCOOP OUT AND MASH THE AVOCADOS Cut the avocados in half lengthwise and remove the seeds. Using a spoon, scoop out all of the flesh and place it in the bowl with the vegetables.

A potato masher or tart tamper is a great tool for this next step. If you don't have either, a dinner fork will do just fine.

Mash the avocado until you achieve the consistency you want.

SEASON WITH LIME JUICE AND SERVE Add the lime juice to the guacamole and combine well. Taste for seasoning and adjust if needed.

Place the guacamole in a serving bowl and garnish with cilantro sprigs.

COOKING NOTES

INGREDIENTS

Hass avocados These are also known as California avocados. They have a rich nutty flavor and a creamy texture. For these recipes, use only fully ripened ones that are completely dark and easily yield to light pressure.

Chipotle chiles These are smoked jalapeños. As such, they are only found dried or canned in adobo sauce. I find that they tend to have a bit more heat than fresh jalapeños. As with any chile, you can decrease the heat by removing the seeds.

TECHNIQUES

Scooping out an avocado Cut the avocado in half by slicing it lengthwise with a large knife. Once you hit the seed in the center, slide your knife along its perimeter to halve the avocado. Open the avocado by gently twisting and pulling on each half. The seed will stay embedded in one half.

Remove the seed by tapping it with the sharp edge of your knife, causing the knife to become wedged into the seed. Twist the knife a bit to dislodge the seed. Use a spoon to scoop out the avocado flesh.

Using a molcajete A *molcajete* is a mortar and pestle made of volcanic rock. If you have one, use it instead of a knife to grind the vegetables to a paste. Place the aromatic ingredients in the bowl and sprinkle with salt, then mash them with the pestle. Fold in and smash the avocado and finish by sprinkling the guacamole with lime juice.

Like cast iron pans, molcajetes tend to be handed down from generation to generation, as they get better with age. Molcajetes are great for making guacamole and sauces, and they also function as beautiful serving pieces. If you purchase a new one, keep in mind you will have to season it following the manufacturer's instructions.

ADVANCE PREPARATION

Guacamole is best eaten right after it has been prepared. If you need to store it for a short period of time, sprinkle some lime juice over it and place a piece of plastic wrap directly on its surface. This will keep the avocado from turning dark for about 1 hour.

CHILE-MARINATED PORK TACOS
WITH PINEAPPLE SALSA {TACOS AL PASTOR}

This is an updated version of tacos al pastor, the pork that is cooked on a rotisserie spit, then rotated upright with a skewered pineapple placed on top of the spit (the technique is similar to that used to cook lamb meat for gyros). The meat continues to cook over low heat as the pineapple juice slowly drips down and flavors the pork. This version, modified for grilling at home, marinates thinly sliced pork with a traditional chile paste. The spicy pineapple salsa brightens up the grilled meat with fresh and vibrant flavors. My neighbors are always peeking over to see what I'm cooking when this meat hits the grill! **Serves 8**

Ancho Chile Paste
8 cloves garlic, peeled
¼ cup packed light brown sugar
¼ cup ancho chile powder
4 canned chipotle chiles in adobo, stemmed
2 teaspoons ground cumin
1 teaspoon black pepper
1 tablespoon dried oregano
2 teaspoons salt
½ cup apple cider vinegar

5 pounds boneless, skinless pork shoulder, cut
    against the grain into ½-inch steaks

Pineapple Salsa
1 pineapple, peeled, cored, sliced, and diced
    small (about 4 cups)
2 serrano chiles, stemmed, seeded (optional), and
    finely chopped
1 red onion, finely chopped (about 1 cup)
1 cup lightly packed cilantro leaves and tender
    stems, chopped
Juice of 2 limes (about 3 tablespoons)
1 teaspoon salt

16 to 20 corn tortillas
3 limes, quartered
Cilantro sprigs, for garnish

COOKING NOTES

INGREDIENTS

Pork shoulder This cut comes from the upper portion of the front legs. It is somewhat fatty, with lots of flavor. Although it's considered a tough cut of meat, if it is cut thinly before cooking, it can be grilled without becoming tough or dry.

Although it can have a thick skin and large bone, pork shoulder can also be purchased in a boneless and skinless cut, which is easiest for cutting up into steaks. If you are using a bone-in shoulder with skin, cut off the skin and cut the meat off around the bone. You will most likely end up with odd-sized chunks and slices of pork. Don't worry about it—just be careful when grilling that the smaller pieces do not overcook.

Serrano chiles Serrano chiles are hotter than jalapeños but milder than habaneros, making them the perfect compromise on heat. Feel free to use the chile of your choice in the quantity of your choice, but don't eliminate the chiles entirely, as it offers a great flavor balance to the sweet pineapple.

PREPARE THE ANCHO CHILE PASTE AND MARINATE THE PORK Using a food processor or blender, puree all the ingredients for the chile paste until smooth.

Place the pork in a large resealable plastic bag (you may need to use two bags) and pour in the marinade. Massage the marinade into the pork, taking care to thoroughly coat all the pieces. Press out as much air as possible from the bag, seal it, and place it in the refrigerator to marinate for at least 30 minutes, or overnight. Make sure you bring the pork to nearly room temperature before grilling.

PREPARE THE SALSA Combine all the ingredients for the salsa in a medium bowl and toss well. Taste for seasoning and adjust if necessary. Set aside

GRILL THE PORK AND TORTILLAS Heat your grill to high (550°F) and close the lid. Wait at least 15 minutes before lowering the heat to medium-high (450°F) and continuing.

Meanwhile, prepare tortilla packets for the grill. Lightly sprinkle each tortilla with water and stack them in batches of about 5 in the center of sheets of aluminum foil. Fold the foil shut into packets and set aside.

Oil the grill grates with a vegetable oil–soaked paper towel held with a long pair of tongs. With marinade still clinging to it, place the pork on the grill. Close the lid and cook for 8 to 10 minutes, or until the underside develops dark, charred grill marks. Lower the heat to medium and turn the pork over. Close the lid and continue cooking for an additional 5 minutes. The meat is ready when both sides of the meat develop charred grill marks. Because the pork is cut so thin, you can rely on its appearance and do not have to bother taking an internal temperature to make sure it is cooked through.

COOKING NOTES

TECHNIQUES

Chopping meat for tacos To make tacos easier to eat by hand, all fillings should be in bite-size pieces. This includes the meat, which should be cut up into $1/2$-inch pieces—irregular shapes are fine.

Choosing a pineapple You cannot tell how sweet a pineapple is by looking at it, because its color it not an indicator of its taste. Look for fruit with bright-looking leaves and avoid any with dark spots on the skin. Because pineapples do not ripen further (get sweeter) after they have been harvested, they are ready to eat as soon as they are picked. They do decrease in acidity over time, which can make them seem to grow somewhat sweeter.

ADVANCE PREPARATION

Most of this recipe can be made in advance. The pork can be marinated and the salsa prepared the night before and left in the refrigerator. The tortilla packets can be assembled a few hours before heating.

Remove the pork from the grill and allow it to rest for 5 minutes. In the meantime, increase the heat to medium-high and wait 5 minutes before continuing. Place the tortilla packets on the grill, close the lid, and heat for 5 minutes. Place the heated tortillas on a dish and keep them warm by placing a hot, damp towel over them.

CHOP THE MEAT AND SERVE Chop the pork into $1/2$-inch pieces. Place on a serving platter and garnish with lime wedges and cilantro sprigs. Serve with the pineapple salsa and warmed tortillas, allowing your guests to assemble their own tacos.

CHIPOTLE-RUBBED SKIRT STEAK TACOS
{TACOS AL CARBON CON CHIPOTLE}

Nothing defines Mexican street food like a taco. Charred meat is tucked inside a soft corn tortilla and layered with vibrant sauces and crunchy toppings. I love to serve these addictive wraps when I'm entertaining in my backyard. Taking inspiration from taco trucks, I set everything out on platters and allow my guests to build their own tacos. It's not only less work for me, but everyone is happy, since they get to eat what, when, and how much they want. **Serves 8**

Chipotle Chile Rub
2 tablespoons chipotle powder
2 tablespoons ancho chile powder
2 tablespoons packed light brown sugar
1 tablespoon ground cumin
2 tablespoons kosher salt

3 pounds skirt steak, trimmed of extra fat and
    cut into pieces that will fit on your grill

Glaze
⅓ cup honey
¼ cup lime juice (from 3 or 4 limes)

32 corn tortillas
1 cup queso fresco or feta cheese, crumbled
Fresh Radish & Cucumber Salad (page 36)
Charred Tomatillo Sauce (page 32)
4 limes, cut into small wedges

RUB THE BEEF WITH THE CHIPOTLE RUB Heat your grill to high (550°F) and close the lid. Wait at least 15 minutes before lowering the heat to medium-high (450°F) and continuing.

Prepare the rub by placing all of the ingredients in a small bowl; mix well to combine and set aside.

About 5 minutes before you are ready to grill, pat the rub all over the steak. I find it helpful to sprinkle some of the rub onto a cutting board and then press the steak onto it, making sure to coat all sides and crevasses of the meat. Allow the beef to rest for about 5 minutes before grilling.

{CONTINUED ON NEXT PAGE}

COOKING NOTES

INGREDIENTS

Chipotle powder Chipotles are smoked jalapeños, so they deliver both smoke and heat (great flavors to grill with). Chipotles are sometimes dried and then ground into a powder; this allows you to use them as a spice. Just keep in mind that chipotle powder packs a fiery punch.

Queso fresco Served with many Mexican dishes, this tangy, salty cow's milk cheese is similar to farmer's cheese. It is purchased as a large disk or wedges and served crumbled. Queso fresco does not melt well. Feta cheese is often used as a substitute.

ADVANCE PREPARATION

The rub can be prepared in advance and stored for weeks, so long as it's kept in an airtight container in the freezer (you will need to break freezer-stored rub apart with your fingers before using). If left at room temperature, the brown sugar will dry out and harden. You will not only have small hard sugar balls in the rub, the meat will not benefit from the sweet flavor.

GRILL THEN GLAZE THE BEEF Oil the grill grates with a vegetable oil–soaked paper towel held with a long pair of tongs.

Place the steak on the grill and cook with the lid open for 3 minutes. Turn the steak over and cook for another 3 minutes with the lid open. Remove the steak from the grill and place on a cutting board. Using the same paper towel–tong system, clean the grill of any spice clumps and reapply vegetable oil.

Prepare the glaze by placing the honey and lime juice in a small bowl and mixing with a fork until well combined. Liberally brush the glaze on one side of the beef and place the meat, glaze side down, onto the grill. Brush more glaze on the top of the steak and allow to cook for 2 minutes.

Turn the steak over and cook for an additional 2 minutes to reach an internal temperature of 125° to 130°F for medium-rare, or continue cooking until you reach your desired level of doneness (see page 10). Keep basting with glaze if you cook the beef longer.

Remove the meat from the grill and set it on a cutting board to rest for at least 5 minutes.

HEAT THE TORTILLAS AND CHOP THE BEEF In the meantime, place the corn tortillas on a dish and cover with a damp paper towel. Heat the tortillas in the microwave for 30 to 60 seconds, until heated through. Alternatively, lightly sprinkle each of the tortillas with water and wrap small batches (about 5 tortillas each) in foil. Heat the foil packets on the covered grill for a few minutes. Place the heated tortillas on a dish and keep warm by placing a hot damp towel over them.

Now chop the beef into bite-size pieces. Begin by slicing the meat into long strips against the grain and then cut those strips crosswise into ½-inch pieces. If you have any remaining glaze, slather some of it on the meat.

SERVE THE TACOS Set out platters and bowls containing the beef, the warmed corn tortillas, crumbled cheese, radish and cucumber salad, tomatillo sauce, and lime wedges and allow your guests to help themselves.

THE BASICS OF TACO ASSEMBLY

1. Start with two corn tortillas. Because tacos are layered with sauces and toppings, the second tortilla serves as insurance in case the first falls apart.

2. Place the meat down the center of the tortilla. Always use well-seasoned meat that is chopped up into bite-size pieces for easy eating.

3. Drizzle on a salsa. Salsas not only provide flavor and moisture, they can also add additional heat.

4. Finish with the topping(s) of your choice. Typical toppings are crumbled cheese (queso fresco), crunchy radishes, pickled onions, and cilantro sprigs.

Citrus- & Oregano-Marinated **SPLIT CHICKEN** {POLLO ENTERO ADOBADO CON JUGO CITRICO Y OREGANO}

If someone asks me to describe quintessential Latin barbecued chicken, I say it's garlicky and tangy with charred, crispy skin. Although this recipe is part of the Mexican chapter, it really could have appeared in any of the others. It's truly finger licking! Whole chickens are cost-effective, and they grill evenly and easily when butterflied, which is much easier to do than it sounds. However, you can certainly use precut chicken; just make sure to use bone-in, skin-on pieces for more flavor. **Serves 8**

Citrus & Oregano Marinade
1 onion, coarsely chopped
10 cloves garlic, peeled
1⅓ cups orange juice (from 3 to 4 oranges)
1⅓ cups lime juice (from about 16 limes)
3 tablespoons dried oregano
2 teaspoons ground cumin
1½ cups lightly packed cilantro leaves and
     tender stems

¼ cup olive oil
2 teaspoons salt
1 teaspoon black pepper

2 (4-pound) whole chickens, split in half, or
     8 pounds bone-in, skin-on chicken parts
2 limes, cut into wedges

{CONTINUED ON NEXT PAGE}

COOKING NOTES

TECHNIQUE

Splitting a whole chicken A split chicken, also referred to as butterflied or spatchcock chicken, is a flattened chicken that has had its backbone and breastbone removed. It's easier to do than it may sound!

Step 1: Remove the backbone While you can use a knife, it's best to use kitchen shears (scissors) for this. Place the chicken on your cutting board back-side facing up, with the tail end and drumsticks close to you. Reach into its cavity and remove the sack of innards and pull away the extra fat from around opening. Holding on to the tail, cut along one side of the backbone (so you are cutting through to the cavity), and then the other. You will hear cracking from the small rib bones that you are cutting through. Discard the bone.

Open the chicken and gently press down on both sides of the breast and thighs to flatten the chicken so that it stays open.

Step 2: Remove the breastbone Rotate the chicken 180 degrees so the wings are close to you.

Use a paring knife to cut a small slit over the cartilage located in the center directly over the breastbone. Pop the breastbone out by bending the breast meat back with your hands. Run your thumb and index finger along the breastbone to separate it from the flesh. The bone should come right out. Discard it.

Step 3: Tuck in the legs Use a paring knife to make a 1-inch slit where the breast ends and the thigh begins. Repeat on the other side. Take a drumstick and pass it through the slit on the same side, making sure to insert the leg through the skin side. The entire leg does not go through, just the top portion. From the skin side of the chicken, the legs will look like they are curled up in a circular pattern. Again, repeat with the other side.

ADVANCE PREPARATION

The citrus marinade can be made up to a couple of days in advance and kept refrigerated. The chicken can be left marinating overnight.

PREPARE THE MARINADE Place all the marinade ingredients in a blender and puree until smooth. Reserve about 1 cup of the marinade as a basting liquid and set aside.

MARINATE THE CHICKENS Pat the chickens dry, place in a deep baking dish, and season all sides with salt and pepper. Pour the marinade over the chickens, making sure all sides are well coated. Allow to marinate at least 1 hour, or overnight.

GRILL THE CHICKENS Heat your grill to high (550°F) and close the lid. Wait at least 15 minutes before continuing.

Oil the grill grates with a vegetable oil–soaked paper towel held with a long pair of tongs. Place the chickens skin side down on the grill. Keeping the heat on high and the lid open, grill for 10 minutes to crisp the skin and render some of the fat. Lower the heat to medium-high (450°F) and baste the chicken with the reserved marinade before turning the chickens over and closing the lid. Cook for another 10 minutes before flipping the chickens a final time. Baste the chicken again and cook for 10 more minutes, or until the leg meat registers 155°F.

When the chickens are ready, the joints will be very loose. You will need a large spatula to remove the chickens from the grill. Allow them to rest for 5 minutes before cutting them up.

SERVE Place the cut-up chicken on a platter and serve with lime wedges.

CREMA

This condiment is a staple in Mexican cooking. It has a thinner consistency than sour cream and a richer flavor. I absolutely love it, and was so relieved when I figured out a way to make my own, since I can't always make it to the specialty store to pick some up. It is a must when you are serving spicy food, as the cream mellows the heat. **Makes 2 cups**

1 cup sour cream
1 cup heavy cream
1 teaspoon salt

MIX THE CREAM AND SALT Combine all the ingredients in a bowl, cover with plastic wrap, and set it out at room temperature for 3 hours.

SERVE OR STORE Transfer to a serving bowl if using right away, or transfer to an airtight container and refrigerate if storing.

COOKING NOTES

ADVANCE PREPARATION

The crema can be made and stored in an airtight container in the refrigerator for as long as the sour cream would last (so pay attention to the sour cream's expiration date). Bring to room temperature before serving.

CHARRED GREEN ONIONS

So simple, yet so delicious! If you like grilled onions but have never grilled green onions before, you will wonder why you never thought of it before. They're easy to maneuver on the grill and are delicious when layered in a taco or just popped into your mouth. **Serves 8**

2 bunches green onions, dark green tops and
    roots trimmed
Canola or olive oil
Salt and black pepper

PREPARE THE GREEN ONIONS Lightly drizzle the green onions with oil and season with salt and pepper.

GRILL THE GREEN ONIONS Heat your grill to high (550°F) and close the lid. Wait at least 15 minutes before lowering the heat to medium-high (450°F) and continuing.

Cut an 8-inch piece of aluminum foil and set aside next to the grill. Place the green onions on the grill and cook for 4 minutes, or until you see grill marks appear on the onions. Flip the onions over and cook for an additional 4 minutes. Place the cut piece of foil on one side of the grill. Using tongs to pick up the onions, place the green tops on the foil (leave the thicker white parts directly on the grill) and continue grilling the onions for an additional 4 minutes per side.

SERVE Remove the onions from the grill, place on a platter, and serve.

COOKING NOTES

INGREDIENTS

Green onions Also referred to as scallions, these are immature onions that are milder tasting than the more mature bulbs. They are identified by their green tops, white roots, and long, thin bodies.

CHARRED TOMATILLO SAUCE

I love tomatillo sauce—its spicy, tangy flavor is incredibly addicting. I used to always make a fresh sauce by pureeing the raw ingredients, until one day I saw a friend grill some tomatillos for his version. I took that method one step farther and grilled the jalapeños and green onions for an even deeper charred flavor. Now I can't decide if I like the fresh or charred sauce better, so I'm giving you recipes for both, and one recipe that also uses avocado (see the Variations, below). **Makes about 2 cups**

10 tomatillos, husks removed, rinsed
2 jalapeño chiles, stemmed and seeded (if desired)
4 green onions, dark green tops and roots trimmed
1 cup lightly packed cilantro leaves and tender stems
½ teaspoon salt

COOKING NOTES

INGREDIENTS

Tomatillos Often mistaken for a green tomato, this fruit, which is actually a member of the gooseberry family, has a fresh, tart flavor. Tomatillos vary in size but average about 2½ inches in diameter. Their size has no relation to their flavor, so pick the freshest-looking ones that are firm with a bright green color and no blemishes.

TECHNIQUE

Cleaning tomatillos Most tomatillos come with a thin paper husk attached. It usually comes off easily, but in the event you get a husk that is difficult to remove, soak the tomatillo in cold water for a minute, and the husk should come right off. Tomatillos tend to have a sticky coating; this is easily cleaned off with a rinse of water.

ADVANCE PREPARATION

This sauce can be made several days in advance with no effect on its color or flavor.

GRILL THE VEGETABLES Heat your grill to high (550°F) and close the lid. Wait at least 15 minutes before continuing.

Oil the grill grates with a vegetable oil–soaked paper towel held with a long pair of tongs. Place the tomatillos, jalapeños, and green onions directly on the grill. Allow the skin of the vegetables to char all over before removing them from the grill, about 4 minutes per side. The total time each vegetable needs may vary. Ultimately you are looking for the skin of each vegetable to be black and blistered all over.

PUREE THE SAUCE AND SERVE Place all the sauce ingredients, including the charred vegetables with skin intact, in a blender and puree until smooth. Transfer to a small bowl and serve.

TOMATILLO SAUCE VARIATIONS

FRESH TOMATILLO SAUCE As an alternative, you can prepare a fresh tomatillo sauce by simply placing all the ingredients in their raw state in a blender and pureeing until smooth.

CREAMY FRESH TOMATILLO SAUCE Add the flesh of a Hass avocado to the blender when preparing the fresh tomatillo sauce. The avocado creates a creamy consistency that pairs famously with charred grilled meats. The sauce will keep for several days in the refrigerator, as the tomatillos' high level of acidity will prevent the avocado from turning dark brown.

GRILLED CORN ON THE COB with Chipotle Crema & Queso Fresco {ELOTE A LA PARILLA}

Just as it does at street fairs, grilled sweet corn will have your guests lining up for their turn. Corn on the cob is steamed in its husks on the grill and then charred to concentrate all its natural sweetness. This is then balanced with a slathering of smoky fire from chipotle crema and a dusting of saltiness from cheese. Pure perfection! Serves 8

8 ears of corn, husks on but silks removed

Chipotle Crema
2 canned chipotle chiles in adobo, stemmed
½ cup crema, homemade (page 30) or store bought

1 cup crumbled queso fresco or feta cheese
2 limes, cut into wedges

SOAK THE CORN Place the corn in a large stockpot or other container large enough to hold all the ears, and fill it with water. If you do not have a sufficiently large container, use your kitchen sink.

Allow the corn to soak for 20 minutes. Remove from the water, shake, and tightly squeeze the husks against the kernels of corn to get rid of any excess water. {CONTINUED}

COOKING NOTES

INGREDIENTS

Using corn without husks You can still make this recipe if the corn you buy comes already husked. Soak the corn in water as is called for in the recipe. Before grilling, wrap the corn tightly in aluminum foil to act as a substitute for the husks. Grill the corn as instructed in the recipe and, when the time comes to char the corn, simply remove and discard the foil.

Canned chipotles Chipotles are smoked jalapeños. The smoking process concentrates their flavor and makes them a bit hotter than regular jalapeños. You can control the heat by keeping or removing the seeds that cause the heat; to remove them, slit open the chiles and scrape out the seeds with your finger.

For this recipe, you want canned chipotles packed in adobo sauce—and remember, you want two chiles from one can, not two cans of chiles!

TECHNIQUES

Removing silks from corn The silks are the thin strings found inside the husks. Since they are inedible, they need to be removed. To do so, gently pull back the husks halfway down the ear of the corn and pull out the silks. It is fine if a few are left behind; they will burn off when you char the kernels. Fold the husks back over the corn and proceed with the recipe.

Tying back the corn husks After the corn has been grilled in the husks, the husks will have dried out. When you pull the husks back to char the kernels, remove two pieces of dried husk and wrap them around the corn husks, tying them into a knot (you may need to be a bit delicate so as not to break the husks). This step is optional but will result in a beautiful presentation.

ADVANCE PREPARATION

The chipotle crema can be made a day in advance and kept refrigerated. The corn can be prepared a few hours in advance up to the point of charring. Because the corn tends to shrivel up and dry out, it is best to char it shortly before serving.

{GRILLED CORN ON THE COB, CONTINUED}

PREPARE THE CREMA Meanwhile, prepare the crema by placing the chipotles and the crema in a food processor and pureeing until well combined. Alternatively, using a knife, finely chop the chipotles and stir them in with the crema. Set aside.

GRILL THE CORN Heat your grill to high (550°F) and close the lid. Wait at least 15 minutes before lowering the heat to medium-high (450°F) and continuing.

Place the corn on the grill rack and grill the ears for 5 minutes. Turn the corn over and grill for another 5 minutes. Remove from the grill and let rest for 5 more minutes. In the meantime, keep your grill on with the lid closed.

PULL BACK THE HUSKS AND CHAR THE CORN Take the grilled ears of corn and pull back the husks, exposing the kernels. Do not remove the husks, though. If possible, tie the husks back (see Cooking Notes).

Increase the grill temperature to high (550°F). Place a sheet of aluminum foil on one side of the hot grill. Place the pulled-back husks over the foil, allowing the exposed kernels to sit on the grill grates. (This is done so the husks don't burn before the corn can char.)

Close the grill lid and allow the kernels to char for about 5 minutes per side, or until they become dark and golden brown on all sides. Remove the corn from the grill and set aside.

SERVE WITH THE GARNISHES You can prepare the corn for your guests by slathering the corn with the chipotle crema, sprinkling a light coating of cheese over it, and finishing with a squeeze of lime, or set the garnishes out and allow your guests to serve themselves.

FRESH RADISH & CUCUMBER SALAD

Fresh radishes and cucumbers are typically used as toppings on tacos to add a crunchy texture, and as a cool reprieve to a hot salsa. I have always marveled at how such a small garnish can have such an impact on the final flavor and texture of a dish. But why limit those crispy vegetables to a garnish? Here I take them one step farther and combine them for a crisp and refreshing salad. **Serves 10**

2 bunches fresh radishes, trimmed and cut into
    thin wedges
1 tablespoon sugar
1 teaspoon salt
1 English cucumber, sliced in half lengthwise
    then crosswise into ¼-inch slices
3 tablespoons lime juice (from 2 to 3 limes)
¼ bunch cilantro (about 12 sprigs)

PREPARE THE RADISHES Place the radishes in a bowl and sprinkle the sugar and salt over them. Toss well. Allow the radishes to sit for 1 hour. Drain the radishes in a colander and rinse with cold water. If time permits, refrigerate before serving.

SEASON AND SERVE Toss the radishes with the cucumbers and drizzle with the lime juice. Place the vegetables on a serving dish and garnish by tucking the cilantro stems under one side.

COOKING NOTES

INGREDIENTS

Cucumbers I like using English cucumbers—the longer ones that come wrapped in plastic—for this recipe since the skin is not waxed and is therefore edible (cucumbers lose their moisture easily and must either be waxed or wrapped in plastic to retain their water content).

TECHNIQUE

Pickling: salt and sugar The point of sprinkling salt and sugar over the radishes is to season them as well as to concentrate their flavor by extracting some of their moisture. Because of this, you will find the radishes sitting in a puddle of liquid before you drain and rinse them.

ADVANCE PREPARATION

The recipe can be made a few hours in advance and kept refrigerated. Just store the cilantro separately, wrapped in a damp paper towel in the refrigerator, until you are ready to serve.

BEER-STEWED BEANS with Chiles
{FRIJOLES BORRACHOS}

While this Mexican version of pork and beans seems like the perfect barbecue side dish, it is also great served on its own with tortilla chips and a dollop of crema. The heat in the chiles is a perfect complement to the meatiness of the beans, and the beer adds a deep, rich flavor to the broth. However you choose to serve the beans, I am sure you will find them delicious! **Serves 8**

1 pound (about 2½ cups) dried pinto beans
24 ounces beer
¼ pound bacon (about 6 slices)
1 onion, chopped
2 cloves garlic, minced
2 poblano chiles, stemmed, seeded (if desired), and chopped
2 jalapeño chiles, stemmed, seeded (if desired), and chopped
3 plum tomatoes, seeded and chopped
1 teaspoon salt
½ cup lightly packed cilantro leaves and tender stems, chopped

SOAK THE BEANS Pick through the beans for any small stones, then rinse them. Place the beans in a large pot and cover with water by an inch. Allow to sit at room temperature about 8 hours, or overnight.

SIMMER THE BEANS IN BEER Drain the beans and return them to the pot. Add the beer, along with 5 cups of water, and bring to a boil. Lower to a simmer and cook, uncovered, for 1 hour.

SAUTÉ THE AROMATIC INGREDIENTS Place a large sauté pan over medium-high heat and add the bacon. Sauté the bacon until it renders all its fat and the bacon loses its pink color and becomes golden brown, about 6 minutes.

Add the onion, garlic, poblano chiles, and jalapeños to the pan and sauté until the vegetables become limp and translucent, about 5 minutes.

{CONTINUED ON NEXT PAGE}

COOKING NOTES

INGREDIENTS

Beer I use a basic Mexican lager for this recipe, but feel free to use the beer of your choice.

Jalapeños The heat in chiles is found in the seeds and interior veins. You can control how spicy the bean dish is by adding more jalapeños (hotter) or removing the seeds and veins of the ones you use (milder).

Salt It is important not to add salt to the beans until they have softened. Adding salt too early in the process will increase the time it takes for the beans to become tender, adding substantially to the cooking time.

TECHNIQUE

Bean quick-soak method If you do not have enough time to soak your beans overnight, place the beans in a pot with enough water to cover by an inch, cover, and bring to a boil for 2 minutes. Remove the pot from the heat and let stand for 1 hour. Then proceed with step two of the recipe, simmering the beans in beer.

Seeding tomatoes To seed tomatoes, cut the tomato into quarters lengthwise (from the stem end), then slice off the seedy pulp, making sure to cut off the core. Plum tomatoes are best in this recipe because they contain fewer seeds and less pulp than the round varieties.

ADVANCE PREPARATION

Not only can this recipe be made a couple of days in advance, its flavors will improve. The beans also freeze well when stored in an airtight container. Just defrost and heat before serving.

Add the tomatoes and salt and cook until the tomato starts to break down, about 3 minutes.

TEST AND SIMMER BEANS Skim off any gray foam that has risen to the surface of the beans. Before you continue with the recipe, the beans must be tender. Test one bean by pinching it between your fingers. If it easily yields to pressure, the beans are ready. If the beans are still tough, continue simmering until they soften. This will require some judgment on your part; you will decide how soft you want the beans to be. If you continue cooking, you do not need to add more liquid; just stir the beans often.

Add the sautéed vegetable and bacon mixture to the beans and continue simmering for another hour to allow the flavors to blend. Control the liquid content by allowing the beans to simmer uncovered (for thicker beans) or covered (for soupy beans).

GARNISH AND SERVE When the beans are done, taste for salt and adjust as necessary. Stir in the cilantro and serve.

MEXICAN CHOCOLATE CUPCAKES with Cajeta Buttercream

Mexican chocolate (dark chocolate flavored with cinnamon and vanilla) and *cajeta* (caramel made from goat's milk) are two baking ingredients that are distinctly Mexican. I was inspired by these two flavors to come up with a dessert that is not only rich and decadent, but also ridiculously simple to prepare, as all the cake ingredients are added to a bowl at the same time and mixed. **Makes 24 cupcakes**

2½ cups all-purpose flour
1¼ cups Dutch-process cocoa powder
2½ cups sugar
2 teaspoons baking soda
1 teaspoon baking powder
1 teaspoon salt
3 eggs
1¼ cups milk
½ cup vegetable oil
1 tablespoon vanilla extract

Cajeta Buttercream
2 sticks (1 cup) unsalted butter, at room temperature
1 cup confectioners' sugar
½ cup cajeta, dulce de leche (see page 139), or caramel sauce

PREPARE THE CAKE BATTER Preheat your oven to 350°F. Line two 12-cup cupcake pans with paper liners.

Combine all the cake ingredients in a large bowl and, using a stand mixer with the paddle attachment or handheld electric mixer, beat on medium speed for 2 minutes until the batter is smooth and shiny. The batter will be a bit thick.

BAKE THE CUPCAKES Transfer the cake batter to a liquid measuring cup for easy pouring and fill the cupcake liners no more than halfway. Bake for 20 to 25 minutes, or until an inserted skewer or toothpick comes out clean.

Remove the cupcake pans from the oven, place on wire racks, and allow to cool completely before frosting.

PREPARE THE CAJETA BUTTERCREAM Using a handheld electric mixer or stand mixer with the paddle attachment, beat the butter, sugar, and cajeta for 3 minutes on medium-high speed, until the frosting is smooth and creamy. Scrape the sides and bottom of the bowl as needed to fully incorporate the cajeta.

ASSEMBLE AND SERVE Remove the cupcakes from the pan and use a spatula to spread the buttercream over the tops of the cupcakes. For a more decorative presentation, you can pipe the buttercream as explained in the Cooking Notes.

COOKING NOTES

INGREDIENTS

Cajeta *Cajeta* (ca-HEH-ta) is a caramel sauce made from goat's milk (or a combination of goat's milk and cow's milk) cooked slowly with vanilla and sugar until a sweet, thick golden-brown syrup is achieved.

While the flavor is a bit different, dulce de leche or regular caramel sauce can be substituted for cajeta in this recipe. Both cajeta and dulce de leche can be purchased at gourmet shops, Latin grocery stores, and some supermarkets.

Dutch-process cocoa powder Cocoa powder is available in two forms: Dutch-process (alkalized unsweetened) and natural unsweetened. The Dutch-process form has a neutral pH and mild flavor. Because pH will affect the leavening action of baking powder, it is important to use the specific type of cocoa that is called for in a recipe.

TECHNIQUE

Creating a piping bag If you do not have a pastry bag to pipe the buttercream with, you can create one with a heavy-duty resealable plastic bag. Simply fill the bag with the buttercream (no more than one-third to half full), pushing the buttercream toward a bottom corner. When you are ready to pipe the frosting, snip off the tip of the corner to create an opening. Carefully squeeze the buttercream through the opening.

ADVANCE PREPARATION

The cupcakes and buttercream can be made a day in advance and stored separately. The cupcakes should be loosely covered with plastic and left at room temperature, while the buttercream needs to be stored in an airtight container in the refrigerator. Allow the buttercream to return to room temperature before beating again so that it is smooth for piping.

Yucatecan Barbecue

Drink

Beer Cocktail / *Michelada* {42}

Starter

Lime-Marinated Shrimp & Crab
Cocktail / *Mariscos en Escabeche* {43}

Main Courses

Chile-Rubbed Tuna Steak with
Avocado & Lime {46}

Achiote-Marinated Chicken Wrapped
in Banana Leaves / *Pollo Pibil* {47}

Yucatecan Barbecue Pork
Spareribs / *Costillitas Pibil* {50}

Condiments & Sides

Marinated Red Onions {52}

Fiery Tomato Salsa / *Xni Pec* {53}

Crunchy Jicama & Lime Salad {54}

Dessert

Grilled Pineapple Skewers
& Pineapple Ice {55}

The Yucatán is a part of southern Mexico located on a large peninsula that juts into the Caribbean Sea. Here, indigenous Mayan customs are fused with Spanish influences. Geographically isolated from the rest of Mexico, the Yucatán has developed a cuisine that is highly influenced by Caribbean and European cultures, and the area's proximity to the Caribbean gives it a tropical feel. Key ingredients of Yucatecan cuisine include tropical fruits and citrus like bitter orange and lime; honey; achiote seeds; chiles; banana leaves; tomatoes; fish and shellfish; and pork and turkey.

{MENU GAME PLAN}

One day in advance:
- Prepare the pineapple ice. Storage: freezer
- Marinate the red onions. Storage: refrigerator

The night before:
- Marinate the chicken. Storage: refrigerator
- Marinate the pork ribs and wrap them in banana leaves and foil. Storage: refrigerator
- Prepare the rub for the tuna. Storage: room temperature

On the morning of:
- Prepare the Lime-Marinated Shrimp & Crab Cocktail. Storage: refrigerator
- Prepare the Fiery Tomato Salsa. Storage: room temperature
- Prepare the Crunchy Jicama & Lime Salad. Storage: refrigerator

Two to three hours before:
- Wrap the chicken in banana leaves. Storage: refrigerator
- Roast the ribs.
- Cut and skewer the pineapple. Storage: room temperature

In the hour before (setup):
- Set up the bar for micheladas.
- Set out:
  Marinated Red Onions
  Fiery Tomato Salsa

As your event unfolds:
- Prepare the micheladas.
- Serve the Lime-Marinated Shrimp & Crab Cocktail.
- Grill the chicken.
- Grill and glaze the pork ribs.
- Place the rub on the tuna and grill.
- Cut the avocado and lime to serve with the tuna.
- Bring out the Crunchy Jicama & Lime Salad.
- Serve the main courses and sides.
- Grill the pineapple skewers.
- Bring out the pineapple ice pan.
- Serve dessert.

BEER COCKTAIL {MICHELADA}

Mexicans love their *cerveza*, or *chela* (slang for beer). It's no wonder they would take their passion one step further and create *cervezas preparadas*, or beer cocktails. The basic cerveza preparada is called a *chelada*: beer plus ice, lime, and salt. There are regional variations in the ingredients, but a *michelada* (which is also considered a good remedy for a hangover) adds Worcestershire sauce and hot sauce to a chelada. **Makes 1 cocktail**

Ice
12 ounces pale Mexican beer
Dash of Worcestershire sauce
Hot sauce
½ lime
Pinch of salt

Fill a chilled pint glass with ice and pour in the beer. Add the Worcestershire sauce, a few dashes of hot sauce, and the juice of the lime. Finish it off with a pinch of salt and serve.

COOKING NOTES

TECHNIQUES

Salt I'm not sure if this was the original purpose for the salt when the michelada was invented, but a dash of salt maintains the beer's fizz.

ADVANCE PREPARATION

A michelada needs to be served right away.

LIME-MARINATED SHRIMP & CRAB COCKTAIL
{MARISCOS EN ESCABECHE}

Also known as *vuelve a la vida* (which literally translates as "come back to life"), this *marisco* is a popular spicy tomato-based seafood cocktail served in Mexican beach towns. Commonly eaten the morning after a night of revelry, it is thought to be restorative. This recipe borrows the spicy and tangy flavors of a bloody Mary and pairs them with the sweet meat of shrimp and crab. It's a great dish with which to start (or end) any party. **Serves 10**

1 pound large shrimp, peeled, deveined, and butterflied
1 pound lump crabmeat
½ red onion, cut in half and sliced very thinly
4 plum tomatoes, seeded and chopped
1 cucumber, peeled, seeded, and chopped
2 jalapeño chiles, stemmed, seeded (if desired), and finely chopped
2 cups lightly packed cilantro leaves and tender stems, chopped
1 cup lime juice (from about 12 limes)
½ cup red wine vinegar
1 cup ketchup
1 tablespoon salt
Sprigs of cilantro, for garnish
Tortilla chips, for serving

BLANCH THE SHRIMP Bring a pot of salted water to a boil. Meanwhile, prepare an ice bath by filling a large bowl with ice and cold water.

Add the shrimp to the boiling water and allow to cook for 1 minute. Remove the shrimp from the pot with a slotted spoon and immediately plunge into the ice bath. Allow the shrimp to cool thoroughly in the ice water, then drain and place on paper towels to absorb some of the water. Transfer the shrimp to a bowl.

COOKING NOTES

TECHNIQUES

Why butterfly the shrimp? While you can get away with skipping this step, I like to slice the shrimp in half lengthwise (butterfly them) before plunging them in boiling water for two reasons. Most importantly, butterflying the shrimp makes them cook more quickly and evenly, thereby preventing them from becoming tough and rubbery from overcooking. It also allows the shrimp to compress into an attractive spiral shape when blanched.

Seeding tomatoes and cucumbers To seed tomatoes, cut the tomato into quarters lengthwise (from the stem end), then slice off the seedy pulp, making sure to cut off the core. Plum tomatoes are best in this recipe because they contain fewer seeds and less pulp than the round varieties.

To seed a cucumber, slice it in half lengthwise and use a small spoon to scoop and scrape out all the seeds found in its center.

ADVANCE PREPARATION

This recipe can be made in its entirety up to 8 hours in advance with little effect on its quality. You can prepare the recipe a day in advance and just hold off on tossing in the cucumbers, tomatoes, and cilantro until an hour or so before serving so they maintain their fresh, crunchy textures.

PREPARE THE CRAB Drain the crab of liquid and pick through it to remove any cartilage. Lightly break up some of the larger lumps of crab, leaving a few chunks intact. Mix the crab with the shrimp.

MARINATE THE INGREDIENTS Add the red onion, tomatoes, cucumber, jalapeños, and half the cilantro to the shellfish and mix until well incorporated.

In a small bowl, combine the lime juice, vinegar, ketchup, and salt and stir until well blended. Add this sauce to the shellfish and vegetables and gently toss until well combined.

Cover the bowl with plastic wrap and refrigerate for 1 to 2 hours.

GARNISH AND SERVE Toss the remaining cilantro into the salad and place on a serving dish. Garnish with sprigs of cilantro and serve with tortilla chips.

CHILE-RUBBED TUNA STEAK with Avocado & Lime

If you are looking for a spice rub with a bold punch of flavor that goes well with fish and shellfish, you've found it. Because the smoky heat of chipotle powder takes center stage, you want to make sure the protein you are using is meaty enough to stand up to the heat. I find tuna is the perfect match. To help tame the heat and balance the flavors of this dish, I like to set up a large platter with avocado slices, lime wedges, and cilantro sprigs and allow my guests to create their perfect plate. **Serves 8**

Chile Rub
¾ cup chipotle chile powder
¼ cup ancho chile powder
4 teaspoons ground cumin
2 tablespoons plus 2 teaspoons dried oregano
4 teaspoons salt
½ teaspoon cayenne pepper

4 pounds tuna, portioned into 8 (1-inch-thick) steaks
3 Hass avocados, sliced and sprinkled with lime juice
5 limes, quartered
Cilantro sprigs, for garnish

PREPARE THE RUB Place all the rub ingredients in a bowl and mix well. Set aside.

HEAT THE GRILL AND PREPARE THE TUNA Heat your grill to high (550°F) and close the lid. Wait at least 15 minutes before continuing.

Place all of the rub on a large plate or cutting board. Working with one tuna steak at a time, gently press the steak onto the rub mix, creating a spice crust on all sides of the fish. Set aside and repeat with the rest of the steaks.

Oil the grill grates with a vegetable oil–soaked paper towel held with a long pair of tongs. Place the tuna steaks on the grill and cook until they reach the desired doneness: on average, a 1-inch steak will take about 2 minutes per side to be cooked rare, and about 3 minutes per side for medium-rare. Keep in mind you are grilling on high heat and the fish will cook quickly.

COOKING NOTES

TECHNIQUES

Slicing an avocado Start by slicing the avocado in half lengthwise with a large knife and, once you hit the seed in the center, move your knife along its perimeter. Open the avocado by gently twisting and pulling on each half.

Remove the seed by tapping it with the sharp edge of your knife, causing the knife to become wedged into the seed. Twist the knife a bit to dislodge the seed from the flesh.

Finally, slice the avocado by taking the tip of your knife and drawing straight lines through the flesh of each avocado half, making sure the tip of the knife reaches the skin of the avocado. The closer the lines, the thinner the slices. Use a spoon to scoop out the sliced avocado.

When to apply the spice rub It's best to apply the spice rub to the fish about 5 minutes before you're ready to grill. The salt in the rub may dry out the fish if you leave it on longer.

ADVANCE PREPARATION

The rub can be prepared in advance and will keep in an airtight container for months.

SERVE Place the tuna on a large platter and garnish with slices of avocado, wedges of lime, and sprigs of cilantro.

ACHIOTE-MARINATED CHICKEN
Wrapped in Banana Leaves {POLLO PIBIL}

This recipe is similar in principle to the Yucatecan pork spareribs on page 50. An achiote marinade is used to flavor and season the chicken, and banana leaves are wrapped around the meat to infuse it with smokiness. Traditionally, the chicken would be placed in an earth oven (*pibe*), but this version only requires you to place it in a covered grill. I've served it intact in the banana leaf (which usually draws applause), but I've also chopped the chicken up with the tomato and onion for a delicious taco filling. However you choose to serve it, I guarantee you will love how straightforward this beautiful and mouthwatering dish is to make. **Serves 8**

Achiote Marinade
¼ cup annatto seeds
1 head garlic, cloves separated and peeled
2 tablespoons salt
2 tablespoons ground cumin
¼ cup dried oregano
1 tablespoon black pepper
¾ cup apple cider vinegar
¾ cup orange juice

8 skinless, boneless chicken breasts (about 3 pounds total)
3 large banana leaves
4 plum tomatoes, cored and sliced
1 red onion, sliced

PREPARE THE MARINADE Place the annatto seeds in a blender and turn on high until the seeds are ground. It's all right if the powder is not evenly ground—just try to get it as fine as you can.

{CONTINUED ON NEXT PAGE}

COOKING NOTES

INGREDIENTS

Banana leaves While these long, wide, sturdy leaves come from the banana tree, they do not produce a banana scent or flavor. Instead, they infuse foods with an unexpected yet wonderful earthy and smoky flavor.

They are most commonly found frozen. To use, just thaw them at room temperature and unfold. Whether you are using fresh or frozen leaves, start by cutting off the spine that runs through each leaf, because it will prevent you from folding the leaf properly. Kitchen scissors work best for trimming the leaves.

The frozen packs come with a good number of banana leaves. After you defrost the package and use the leaves that you need, repack the leaves airtight in plastic wrap and return to the freezer. You can defrost and refreeze these hearty leaves as often as you need to without affecting their flavor or texture.

While you will sacrifice a bit of flavor, you can successfully substitute aluminum foil for the banana leaves.

Annatto seeds See the Cooking Notes in Yucatecan Barbecue Pork Spareribs (page 50).

TECHNIQUE

Grilling packets These packets create an environment where the chicken is steamed. After 25 minutes, the chicken will be cooked through and infused with the smoky scent of the banana leaves and the deep red color of the annatto seeds, but it will not have charred flesh or grill marks.

ADVANCE PREPARATION

The chicken can be left marinating overnight. The packets can be assembled and left in the refrigerator for several hours before grilling. Make sure to bring the packets to room temperature before grilling.

Place the remaining marinade ingredients in the blender and puree until all the ingredients are well blended into a paste. Remove the marinade from the blender jar and set aside.

Place the chicken breasts in a large resealable plastic bag (you may need to use two) and pour in the marinade. Make sure to coat the chicken well with the marinade. Press out as much air as possible from the bag, seal it, and refrigerate for at least 45 minutes, or overnight.

PREPARE THE BANANA LEAF PACKETS Use kitchen scissors to cut eight pieces of banana leaves, each approximately 12 inches by 12 inches. Reserve any extra scraps of leaves to make ties.

Remove the marinated chicken from the refrigerator. Lay a banana leaf square in front of you, making sure the shiny side is facing up. Place the chicken breast, with marinade still clinging to it, in the center of the leaf and top it with 3 or 4 slices of tomato and several onion slices.

Fold one side of the leaf over the chicken. Overlap the opposite side over the leaf. Fold the two ends in toward the center and place the package on a baking sheet seam side down. Tear a long strip from an extra piece of banana leaf and tie it around the chicken-stuffed package to secure it. Repeat with the remaining chicken.

GRILL THE PACKETS Heat your grill to high (550°F) and close the lid. Wait at least 15 minutes before lowering the heat to medium-high (450°F) and continuing.

Place the banana leaf packets on the grill, close the lid, and cook for 25 minutes. The leaves will turn dark brown and have a burnt appearance. They will also begin to give off a smoky scent.

SERVE Pile the banana leaf packets on a serving platter and allow your guests to serve themselves and unwrap their packages.

YUCATECAN BARBECUE PORK SPARERIBS
{COSTILLITAS PIBIL}

The Yucatán is known for barbecues that use earth ovens to cook the meat. Pits (called *pibes*) are dug in the ground and lined with rocks and coal. Achiote-marinated meat is then wrapped in fragrant banana leaves, placed in the pit, and covered with a fibrous material similar to burlap before the displaced dirt is used to cover the "oven." To save you from having to dig a ditch I created this recipe, which still infuses the meat with the flavors of the peppery and tart achiote marinade and smoky banana leaves, while relying on your grill to do the cooking. **Serves 8**

6 pounds (3 or 4 racks) pork spareribs
4 large banana leaves, trimmed
Achiote Marinade (page 47)

Glaze
½ cup honey
⅓ cup apple cider vinegar
½ teaspoon cayenne pepper

PREPARE AND MARINATE THE RIBS Make sure the bottom (bony side) of the ribs is lightly scored with small gashes. If it's not, cut shallow 1-inch-long gashes all along the bottoms of the racks. This helps the ribs cook evenly.

Cut a piece of aluminum foil that is about 6 inches longer than a rack of ribs and place it on your work surface. Trim a piece of banana leaf approximately the same length as the foil (don't worry about the width; just make sure the length is about the same), and place it directly over the aluminum foil. Place the ribs, bony side up, on the center of the banana leaves and slather the meat with the marinade. Turn the ribs over and coat well with more marinade.

Close the packet by folding the sides of the banana leaf over the ribs and then wrapping the foil around the leaf, making sure to seal it well. Repeat the same procedure with the remaining racks.

Allow to marinate in the refrigerator for at least 1 hour, or up to 24 hours.

COOKING NOTES

INGREDIENTS

Annatto seeds Also known as achiote seeds, these are the seeds of the achiote tree, and they impart a musky, peppery flavor in addition to a deep red color.

Grind these small, hard seeds in a spice grinder or blender. While ground versions exist, the flavor is not the same and they should only be used as a last resort. You may also find achiote paste, which is ground annatto mixed with vinegar and some other seasonings. You can use this as a starter for the marinade—just check the ingredient label and adjust the recipe proportions accordingly. I start by checking whether oregano and cumin are listed in the label; add the amount in the recipe if they are missing. The next step will take some judgment from you. If you feel the paste is too tart, add a few tablespoons of orange juice. If it's too sweet, add some apple cider vinegar.

Banana leaves See page 48.

ADVANCE PREPARATION

The majority of this recipe can be made well in advance. The marinade and glaze can be stored in the refrigerator in airtight containers for up to a week. The ribs can be marinated, wrapped in the banana leaf–foil packets, and refrigerated overnight.

The ribs can also be roasted 3 to 4 hours in advance, leaving only the glazing to be done before serving.

ROAST THE RIBS Preheat the oven to 275°F. Remove the rib packets from the refrigerator.

Place the packets on a baking sheet and roast in the oven for 2 hours. Remove the tray from the oven and allow the ribs to rest for at least 10 minutes so they have a chance to cool.

GLAZE THE RIBS Heat your grill to high (550°F) and close the lid. Wait at least 15 minutes before lowering the heat to medium-high (450°F) and continuing.

In a small mixing bowl, combine the honey, vinegar, and cayenne pepper until well blended. Set aside.

Oil the grill grates with a vegetable oil–soaked paper towel held with a long pair of tongs.

Carefully open the foil and banana leaf packets, exposing the tops of the rib racks. Brush the ribs with glaze and transfer to the grill, glazed side down. Some of the ribs may be so tender that they fall apart. If that happens, don't worry about it; simply continue with the recipe. Brush the bony side of the ribs (this side should be facing up) with more glaze.

Allow the glaze to caramelize for about 4 to 5 minutes before turning the racks over and cooking for another 4 minutes. Remove the ribs from the grill and allow to rest for 5 minutes before slicing into individual ribs. If you have any extra glaze, dab some on the ribs before serving.

MARINATED RED ONIONS

Pickled onions are a popular condiment throughout the Yucatán, where they are used as a topping for all sorts of grilled meats, seafood, and vegetables. This recipe, which marinates the onions instead of pickling them, delivers the same piquant result with far less fuss. And as soon as you discover how deliciously tangy and ridiculously easy these onions are to make, you will find yourself keeping a container of them in your refrigerator to add to your salads, sandwiches, and grilled meats. Don't be alarmed by how much vinegar you will be using; you can reuse the vinegar for other cooking needs after you have eaten (devoured!) the onions. **Makes about 2 cups**

1 red onion, thinly sliced
2 to 3 cups red wine vinegar

MARINATE THE ONION Place the onion slices in a small bowl or resealable plastic bag and pour in enough red wine vinegar to completely submerge them. If you're using a plastic bag, press out as much air as possible and seal the bag. If you're using a bowl, place a piece of plastic wrap directly on the surface of the onions and vinegar to help keep the onions submerged.

Set the onions aside for at least 20 minutes or up to several days in the refrigerator.

COOKING NOTES

INGREDIENTS

Selecting the onions and vinegar I prefer using a red onion for both its sweet flavor and red color, and I like pairing it with red wine vinegar for the punch of color it creates. However, feel free to use whatever onion you prefer or have available and, with the exception of balsamic vinegar, you can use the vinegar of your choice.

TECHNIQUE

Slicing an onion In order to get thin, evenly sliced onions, it's best to slice the onion from root to stem. Simply cut the onion in half through its roots and peel off its skin. Trim off the roots and the stem end, place one of the cut sides in front of you, and slice the onion lengthwise (you will be going in the same direction as the natural ridges found on the onion).

ADVANCE PREPARATION

This recipe can be done well in advance—it will keep refrigerated for 1 week.

FIERY TOMATO SALSA {XNI PEC}

This is not your everyday tomato salsa— it is something far more serious. *Xni pec* (SHNEE-pek), Mayan for "dog's nose," gets its name from how it makes your nose run. The tomato and cilantro take a back seat to the very hot habanero and jalapeño chiles, both of which are finely minced with seeds and veins intact, making for an incredibly hot and tangy sauce that goes perfectly with all types of grilled meats. If you like it hot . . . knock yourself out! **Makes about 1½ cups**

2 jalapeño chiles, stemmed and minced
3 habanero chiles, stemmed and minced
2 plum tomatoes, cored and finely chopped
2 green onions, roots and dark green tops
    trimmed, finely chopped
3 tablespoons lime juice (from 2 or 3 limes)
½ cup lightly packed cilantro leaves and tender
    stems, chopped
¼ teaspoon salt, plus more to taste

PREPARE THE SALSA Place all the ingredients in a bowl and toss well. Taste for seasoning and add more salt as needed.

┌─ COOKING NOTES ─────────────

INGREDIENTS

Habanero chile One of the hottest chiles used in the kitchen, the habanero is believed to have originated somewhere on the Yucatán Peninsula. Its name refers to the Cuban capital of Havana (spelled *Habana* in Spanish), as it was traded there.

Habaneros are short (about 1½ inches long) and round, and are typically red or orange in color. Habaneros' thin skin and flesh is very similar to those of Scotch bonnet chiles, which can be substituted in this recipe.

ADVANCE PREPARATION

The salsa can be prepared several hours before serving and left in the refrigerator or at room temperature.

CRUNCHY JICAMA & LIME SALAD

Crunchy and tangy with a hint of sweetness is how I would describe this salad. Because I always love to have something crunchy on my plate, this has become a favorite of mine when I'm entertaining outdoors. I also love that jicama's cream-colored flesh will not turn a dull color or lose its crispness even after sitting out for a few hours. **Serves 10**

2½ pounds jicama, peeled and cubed
¼ cup lightly packed cilantro leaves and tender
　　stems, chopped, plus extra sprigs for garnish
½ teaspoon salt
Zest of 1 lime
3 tablespoons lime juice (from 2 or 3 limes)

MARINATE THE JICAMA Place all the ingredients except the cilantro sprigs in a bowl and toss well. Cover and refrigerate for 20 minutes to chill through.

GARNISH AND SERVE Transfer the jicama to a serving dish and drizzle all the remaining marinating liquid over it. Garnish with sprigs of cilantro.

COOKING NOTES

INGREDIENTS

Jicama A starchy root vegetable from a vine of the same name, jicama is very popular in Mexico and can be cooked or eaten raw. It has a very thin, inedible skin and a cream-colored flesh whose appearance and texture are similar to those of apples or pears, but it will not turn brown after it has been cut. Jicama has a sweet flavor that is enhanced by a sprinkling of lime juice or other acid.

TECHNIQUE

Peeling and cutting jicama After cutting off the two flat ends of the jicama, you may notice that the thin skin peels right off. However, I like to cut off the skin with a knife to make sure it all comes off. After that, you can cut the jicama as you would a potato.

ADVANCE PREPARATION

This recipe will benefit from advance preparation, to allow the lime juice to marinate the jicama. It can be made several hours in advance—even the night before—without impact to the vegetable's texture or flavor. Just keep it refrigerated until ready to serve.

GRILLED PINEAPPLE SKEWERS & PINEAPPLE ICE

Pineapple is very popular in the coastal beach towns of Mexico, especially those of the Yucatán. The street vendors who sell skewers of grilled meat and bags of chilled pineapple inspired this refreshing dessert. After discovering how delicious grilled fruit is, I began grilling pineapple skewers to serve with the pineapple ice, and the combination is now one of my favorite summertime desserts. Serves 8 to 10

½ cup sugar
2 cups water
2 pineapples, cored and chopped (about 6 cups)
2 limes, quartered

PREPARE A SIMPLE SYRUP Combine the sugar and water in a saucepan over medium heat. Stir until the sugar has completely dissolved. Remove from the heat and allow the syrup to cool.

PUREE THE PINEAPPLE AND FREEZE Puree half the pineapple chunks (about 3 cups) in a blender until smooth. Pour the simple syrup and pineapple puree in a 9 by 13-inch nonreactive baking pan and stir well. Cover the pan with plastic wrap and place in the freezer.

After one hour, stir the mixture well with a fork. Return to the freezer and allow the mixture to freeze for at least 6 hours or overnight.

SKEWER AND GRILL THE PINEAPPLE Heat your grill to high (550°F) and close the lid. Wait at least 15 minutes before lowering the heat to medium-high (450°F) and continuing.

Oil the grill grates with a vegetable oil–soaked paper towel held with a long pair of tongs. Skewer 2 or 3 of the remaining pineapple chunks onto each of 8 to 10 skewers, placing peices of the same size on each skewer. Grill each skewer for 2 minutes per side, or until you see grill marks develop. Remove from the heat and set aside.

PREPARE THE PINEAPPLE ICE AND SERVE Remove the pan from the freezer and allow it to sit at room temperature for about 5 minutes. Using a fork, scrape the fruit ice into individual serving cups and garnish by spearing a skewer into it and adding a lime wedge.

COOKING NOTES

INGREDIENTS

Simple syrup Simple syrup is sugar that is dissolved in water, but it has to be heated enough so that the sugar actually dissolves. This will prevent the ice from taking on a gritty texture.

Lime The lime is used as both a garnish and a seasoning. The acid in the lime brightens up the flavor of the pineapple and balances its sweetness.

TECHNIQUE

Soaking wooden skewers See page 10.

ADVANCE PREPARATION

This is definitely a recipe to start ahead of time. The pineapple ice can be made several days in advance. You can even scrape the ice early, placing it in an airtight plastic container in the freezer; let it soften for a few minutes before serving. (You may have to scrape it a bit again.) In order to prevent freezer burn, I wrap the container in plastic wrap before placing it in the freezer. The grilled pineapple can sit at room temperature for a few hours.

Nicaraguan Ranch Roast

Drink

Rum & Guava Cooler {58}

Starter

Grilled Ripe Plantains with Crema /
Maduros a la Parilla con Crema {59}

Main Courses

Nicaraguan Grilled Skirt Steak /
Churrasco Nicaragüense {60}

Coffee-Rubbed Cowboy Rib-Eyes {63}

Condiments & Sides

Chunky Fresh Tomato Sauce /
Pico de Gallo {64}

Rice Cooked in Red Beans /
Gallo Pinto {65}

Mixed Green Salad {66}

Dessert

Three Milks Cake / *Tres Leches* {67}

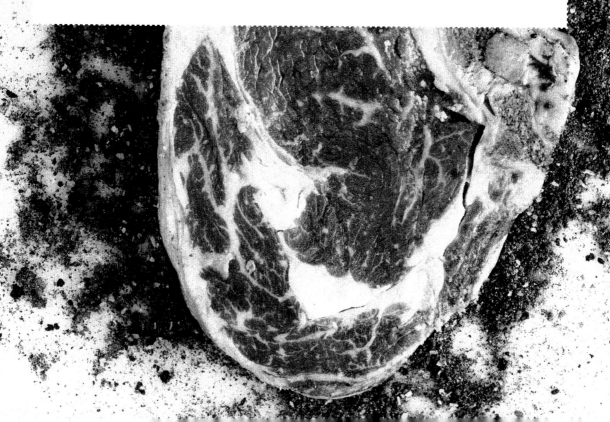

Nicaraguan cuisine reflects a combination of influences, primarily those of pre-Colombian Indians and Spanish colonizers. Farming is a big industry in Nicaragua, with coffee, banana, and tobacco plantations scattered throughout the country. Coffee exports bring in the most revenue, but Nicaragua is also the largest exporter of beef in Central America. Beef and coffee are very important ingredients in the national cuisine, as are rice, beans, plantains, garlic, parsley, and tomatoes.

{MENU GAME PLAN}

One day in advance:
- Bake the yellow cake for the Tres Leches. Cover with plastic wrap. Storage: room temperature

The night before:
- Prepare the three milks mixture and soak the cake. Storage: refrigerator
- Prepare the coffee rub. Storage: freezer
- Prepare the Chimichurri. Storage: refrigerator

On the morning of:
- Trim and marinate the skirt steak. Storage: refrigerator
- Prepare the Gallo Pinto. Storage: room temperature in a covered pot
- Prepare the meringue and top the cake. Storage: refrigerator
- Prepare the glaze for the plantains. Storage: room temperature; will harden and need reheating

Two to three hours before:
- Prepare the salad greens and cover them with a damp towel. Storage: refrigerator
- Prepare the salad dressing. Storage: room temperature
- (Optional) Brulée the meringue on the cake.
- Prepare the Pico de Gallo, but don't add salt yet. Storage: room temperature

In the hour before (setup):
- Set up the beverage bar with the ingredients for the rum coolers.
- Bring the meats to room temperature.
- Set out:
Chimichurri to be used as sauce (1½ cups)
Pico de Gallo

As your event unfolds:
- Prepare the Rum & Guava Coolers.
- Grill the plantains.
- Season the Pico de Gallo with salt and set out.
- Place the rub on the rib-eyes.
- Grill the skirt steak.
- Grill the rib-eyes.
- Bring out the Gallo Pinto.
- Dress the salad.
- Serve the main courses and sides.
- Serve dessert.

RUM & GUAVA COOLER

If you are looking for a cool and refreshing cocktail, you've found it. Made with only four ingredients, this is like a simple yet sophisticated Rum Runner. It's the cocktail I go for on a breezy summer day when the sun is setting. **Makes 1 cocktail**

Ice
2 ounces guava juice
2 ounces light rum
1 ounce fresh lime juice
Sparkling water or club soda
1 lime wedge

Fill a tall glass with ice and set aside. Place a handful of ice in a cocktail shaker and add the guava juice, rum, and lime juice and shake vigorously for 10 to 15 seconds. Strain the cocktail into the glass of ice and top with sparkling water or club soda. Garnish with a lime wedge and serve.

COOKING NOTES

INGREDIENTS

Guava juice Guava is very common in the Caribbean and Central America. Because the fruit is high in pectin, it is often used for jellies and preserves. However, its juice, which is sweet yet tart, is also very popular. If you cannot find guava juice, substitute cranberry juice.

GRILLED RIPE PLANTAINS with Crema
{MADUROS A LA PARRILLA CON CREMA}

If you are not accustomed to eating something sweet with your grilled beef, you are in for a pleasant surprise. These grilled plantains become caramelized with the brown-sugar-and-butter glaze that is slathered over them as they cook, making them a perfect complement to char-grilled beef. In fact, they're so lusciously sweet, I'm never sure whether to serve them as a side dish or a dessert! Serves 8

3 tablespoons unsalted butter
¾ cup packed brown sugar
2 tablespoons apple cider vinegar or sherry vinegar
4 very ripe (black) plantains
1½ cups crema, homemade (page 30) or store bought

PREPARE THE BUTTER GLAZE Place the butter and sugar in a small saucepan over medium heat and cook for about 2 minutes, until the butter has melted completely. Add the vinegar and stir well. Remove from the heat and set aside.

PREPARE AND GRILL THE PLANTAINS Heat your grill to high (550°F) and close the lid. Wait at least 15 minutes before lowering the heat to medium-high (450°F) and continuing. Oil the grill grates with a vegetable oil–soaked paper towel held with a long pair of tongs.

Slice the unpeeled plantains in half lengthwise and place cut side down on the grill. Close the lid and cook for 15 minutes. Turn the plantains over and baste the cut sides with the butter glaze. Close the lid and continue cooking for another 15 minutes. Brush a bit more glaze on the plantains before removing them from the grill.

SERVE Serve the plantains in their skins with the crema in a bowl on the side. When ready to eat, place a dollop of crema over each plantain half.

COOKING NOTES

INGREDIENTS

Plantains Plantains are large starchy bananas and must be cooked before eating. You will find them in various stages of ripeness. For this recipe and for all recipes asking you to use ripe plantains, you want the fruit's skin to be completely black and look like it is rotting (it's not!). Surprisingly, despite its outward appearance, the flesh will be sturdy.

Crema Crema is a thin sour cream served throughout Central America and Mexico. It is as commonly used on sweet as on savory items. If you cannot find it, you can make your own (page 30) or substitute crème fraîche; don't substitute regular sour cream.

ADVANCE PREPARATION

You can prepare the butter glaze a few hours in advance. However, it will thicken at room temperature, requiring you to reheat it.

NICARAGUAN GRILLED SKIRT STEAK
{CHURRASCO NICARAGÜENSE }

Churrasco is a term used throughout Latin America to refer to a thin piece of grilled meat. In Nicaragua, churrasco is made from beef tenderloin that is sliced lengthwise to produce long, thin steaks, which are then marinated in *chimichurri* (fresh parsley sauce). Some skip the butchering step and use skirt steak instead. This is my preference, since skirt steak is already thin and has a delicious beefy flavor that pairs incredibly well with the garlicky chimichurri—some of which is used to marinate the steak while some is reserved to use as a sauce for the cooked steak. The oil-based chimichurri also helps to produce the desirable charred crust on the steak. However, flare-ups can quickly turn it into singed beef, so pay attention at the grill! **Serves 8**

3 pounds skirt steak, trimmed of extra fat
3½ cups Chimichurri (page 152)

MARINATE THE STEAK If desired, cut the large skirt steak into smaller steaks. Place the steak in a resealable plastic bag or deep bowl and pour 2 cups of the chimichurri over it, making sure to coat all surfaces of the meat. If using a plastic bag, press out as much air as possible before sealing the bag. If using a bowl, place a piece of plastic wrap directly on the surface of the meat and marinade, creating an airtight cover. Allow the meat to marinate for at least 1 hour.

GRILL THE STEAK Preheat the grill to its highest temperature, close the lid, and wait 15 minutes. Oil the grill grates with a vegetable oil–soaked paper towel held with a long pair of tongs.

Remove the steaks from the marinade, letting the excess marinade drip off, and place on the grill. Lower the heat to medium-high, close the lid, and cook for 4 minutes. If you tend to get flare-ups on your grill, you may want to leave the lid open; this will result in a longer cooking time. Turn the steaks over and cook for another 4 minutes to reach an internal temperature of 125° to 130°F for medium-rare, or until it reaches the desired doneness (see chart on page 10).

COOKING NOTES

TECHNIQUE

Because this is an oil-based marinade, flare-ups may occur. Review the section on dealing with flare-ups on page 9.

ADVANCE PREPARATION

The chimichurri can be made a day in advance and will keep, refrigerated, for about a week. The steaks can be left marinating for several hours before grilling.

SERVE Place the remaining 1½ cups of chimichurri in a small bowl and serve with the grilled skirt steak.

COFFEE-RUBBED COWBOY RIB-EYES

Many people are surprised when they hear that the first ingredient in this rub is instant espresso powder. While it may seem unorthodox, the coffee conveys a deep, rich flavor that accentuates the beef's meaty essence. The rest of the rub ingredients are there to season the beef, not flavor it: the combination results in an incredibly tasty steak. **Serves 8**

Coffee Rub
6 tablespoons instant espresso powder
2 tablespoons Spanish paprika
1 tablespoon kosher salt
2 teaspoons black pepper
¼ cup packed brown sugar
2 teaspoons garlic powder
2 teaspoons ground cumin

8 (1-pound) bone-in rib-eye steaks
Vegetable oil

PREPARE THE RUB AND PUT IT ON THE MEAT Place all the rub ingredients in a bowl and stir until well combined.

Sprinkle about ¼ cup of the spice blend onto your cutting board and put the steak on it, pressing down. Lift the steak and press down on areas to which the rub has not yet adhered. Turn the steak over and press it down to completely coat the other side. When you are done, you should not be able to see any meat through the spices. Set aside and repeat with the remaining steaks, adding more spice rub to the board as necessary.

Allow the steaks to rest for about 10 minutes before grilling.

{**CONTINUED ON NEXT PAGE**}

COOKING NOTES

INGREDIENTS

Cowboy rib-eye Bone-in rib-eye steak is also called cowboy rib-eye. Rib-eye is known for its marbling and juiciness. I think it goes really well with this rub, but I have also used the rub on sirloin and skirt steak with equal success—so use your favorite cut of meat.

Instant espresso powder Instant espresso powder is brewed espresso that has been dehydrated. As a result, it will quickly give off its flavor. Regular ground espresso beans will not provide much flavor and should not be substituted. As an alternative, use instant coffee.

Paprika Paprika is a spice made from ground dried red bell peppers. Depending on the variety of the pepper, the flavor of the spice can range from hot and spicy to sweet or smoky. Paprika is produced in a few countries, including Spain and Hungry; although Spain was the first country to produce it, Hungarian paprika is considered by many to be superior. I like using a mild Spanish paprika for this recipe, but feel free to use the one you prefer.

TECHNIQUE

Storing extra rub Because this rub contains brown sugar, take a little extra care when storing—it needs to be kept in the freezer so that the sugar does not dry out and become clumpy. Don't be surprised if the frozen spices harden; they just need a few minutes to defrost.

ADVANCE PREPARATION

The rub can be made several days in advance. Refer to Technique, above, for proper storing instructions.

GRILL THE MEAT Heat your grill to high (550°F) and close the lid. Wait at least 15 minutes before continuing.

Oil the grill grates with a vegetable oil–soaked paper towel held with a long pair of tongs. Make sure to have an instant-read thermometer nearby to check the internal temperature of your meat.

Place your steaks on the grill, making sure not to crowd the grill (it's best to flip the steaks over onto a clean area of the grate). Close the lid, decrease the heat to medium-high, and grill the steaks for 5 minutes per side, to an internal temperature of 125 to 130°F for medium rare.

SERVE Remove the steaks from the grill when they are 10 degrees under your desired temperature (see the chart on page 10). Allow them to rest for 5 minutes before serving or slicing.

CHUNKY FRESH TOMATO SAUCE {PICO DE GALLO}

This sauce is very common throughout Central America. Pico de gallo, which literally translates to "rooster's beak," is named for the haphazard chopping of all of the sauce's ingredients—as if a rooster did it with its beak. Unlike its Mexican cousin, the Nicaraguan version does not contain hot chile. It's typically used to accompany grilled meats and chicken. **Serves 8**

2 large tomatoes, chopped
¼ cup finely chopped red onion
½ cup lightly packed cilantro leaves and tender
    stems, finely chopped
1 lime
¼ teaspoon salt

COMBINE ALL INGREDIENTS AND SERVE Place all the ingredients in a bowl and mix until well combined. Serve.

--- COOKING NOTES ---

ADVANCE PREPARATION

You can prepare the sauce a few hours in advance so long as you do not add the salt until you are ready to serve. The salt will cause the vegetables to wilt and turn soggy. Keep the saltless sauce in the refrigerator.

RICE COOKED IN RED BEANS {GALLO PINTO}

Considered the national dish of Nicaragua, *gallo pinto* literally translates as "spotted rooster," a reference to the dish's appearance. The meaty red beans and smoky bacon flavor make this a very satisfying and comforting dish that goes well with almost everything. **Serves 8 to 10**

¼ pound (about 6 slices) bacon, chopped
2 tablespoons olive oil
1 onion, finely chopped (about 1 cup)
1 green pepper, stemmed, seeded, and finely diced (about ¾ cup)
2 cloves garlic, minced
2 tablespoons tomato paste
2 teaspoons salt
1 teaspoon ground cumin
1 teaspoon ground oregano
2 cups long-grain white rice
2 (15½-ounce) cans red kidney beans, not drained
1¾ cups water

RENDER THE BACON FAT Place the bacon and olive oil in a large pot and set it over medium-high heat. Sauté the bacon until it renders its fat and turns a golden brown color, about 6 minutes. Move the bacon around to prevent it from sticking to the bottom of the pot.

SAUTÉ THE VEGETABLES AND RICE Add the onion, green pepper, and garlic to the bacon and sauté until the vegetables are limp and translucent, about 5 minutes. Add the tomato paste, salt, cumin, oregano, and rice and stir for 1 minute, until all the ingredients are well mixed and the rice is coated in oil.

> **COOKING NOTES**
>
> **TECHNIQUE**
>
> **Cooking the rice** Rice requires a specific amount of liquid to cook properly. Because onions and green peppers can contribute a considerable amount of liquid to a recipe, a volume measure for each is given. While the measurements are approximate, making sure the chopped vegetables are close to these amounts will ensure that the rice cooks properly.
>
> **ADVANCE PREPARATION**
>
> You can prepare the recipe in its entirety the night before with very little effect on its taste and texture. However, you will want to warm the dish before serving. This can be done in the microwave or on the stovetop. Just sprinkle about ¼ cup of water over the rice to make sure it does not dry out when reheated.

ADD THE BEANS AND SIMMER Add the beans and their liquid, along with the water, to the pot. Bring to a boil, cover, and reduce to a simmer. Cook for 35 to 40 minutes, or until all the water has been absorbed by the rice.

Allow the covered pot to sit off the heat for 5 minutes. Fluff the rice with a fork and serve.

MIXED GREEN SALAD

I find that a simple green salad is often overlooked by hosts but, when it is offered, it's rarely passed over by guests. A well-made green salad not only adds some needed green to a table, it also complements grilled meats incredibly well. I consider it the little black dress of vegetables: everyone should have a green salad recipe in their repertoire and should feel comfortable whipping it up at a moment's notice. **Serves 10**

Sherry Vinaigrette
2 tablespoons sherry vinegar
2 tablespoons red wine vinegar
2 tablespoons olive oil
Pinch of salt

2 heads butter lettuce, cores removed and leaves
    torn into bite-size pieces
1 pint cherry tomatoes, halved
1 English cucumber, cut in half lengthwise then
    sliced crosswise
2 tablespoons chopped chives

PREPARE THE VINAIGRETTE Place the ingredients for the dressing in a bowl or jar and stir or shake well. Keep in mind that the oil and vinegar will not blend. Set aside.

PREPARE THE SALAD Toss the salad ingredients and place on a serving dish, distributing them evenly.

SERVE When serving large groups in situations where the food will be left out for a while, I like to serve the dressing on the side and allow my guests to drizzle it onto their salads themselves—this keeps the salad greens crisper longer.

Because this dressing is "broken"—that is, the oil and vinegar are not blended—it's important that it be well stirred or shaken before it is served.

COOKING NOTES

INGREDIENTS

Sherry vinegar Like balsamic vinegar, sherry vinegar is aged and, as a result, has a touch of sweetness and a depth of flavor. I like it for both its flavor and its amber color, which looks beautiful when pooled on a dish.

TECHNIQUE

Tearing lettuce leaves Cutting lettuce leaves with a knife will speed up oxidation and cause the edges of the leaf to turn limp and dark. To prevent this, tear the lettuce leaves by hand.

ADVANCE PREPARATION

The dressing can be made well in advance and kept refrigerated in a covered container. Any extra dressing can be kept in the same fashion for a little over a week. You can prepare the salad a few hours in advance so long as you place a damp paper towel over the greens, cover the entire dish with plastic, and place it in the refrigerator.

BASICS OF A WELL-MADE GREEN SALAD:

1. Freshly hand-torn green lettuce leaves.

2. A small amount of chopped herbs to add a layer of flavor and freshness.

3. A well-seasoned vinaigrette dressing—salt balances the flavors.

THREE MILKS CAKE {TRES LECHES}

While *tres leches* is served all over Latin America, Nicaragua is the country that can claim this dish as its own. A plain vanilla cake is soaked in a mixture made from three kinds of milk—evaporated, sweetened condensed, and whole—and then topped with silky meringue. It's a simple yet satisfying dessert, especially when served with a shot of espresso. The recipe for this yellow cake belonged to my great-grandmother Wiwa and is a great basic cake recipe. **Serves 12 to 14**

Cake
2 sticks (1 cup) unsalted butter, at room
    temperature
2 cups sugar
4 eggs
3 cups cake flour
1 tablespoon baking powder
1 teaspoon salt
1 cup milk
1 teaspoon vanilla extract

Milk Mixture
1½ cups whole milk
2½ cups (two 14-ounce cans) sweetened
    condensed milk
3 cups (two 12-ounce cans) evaporated milk

Meringue
4 egg whites
1 cup sugar
Pinch of salt

PREPARE THE CAKE BATTER Preheat the oven to 350°F. Grease the bottom and sides of a 9 by 13-inch baking dish and set aside.

Using a stand mixer with the paddle attachment or a handheld electric mixer, beat the butter and sugar on medium-high speed until the mixture is pale yellow and fluffy, 2 to 4 minutes depending on your mixer. Add the eggs and continue beating until the mixture is light and fluffy, another 3 minutes. Scrape the sides and bottom of the bowl with a rubber spatula if necessary.

Mix the cake flour, baking powder, and salt in a bowl and stir to combine with a whisk or fork.

Combine the milk and vanilla extract in a liquid measuring cup.

With the mixer on medium speed, add a quarter of the flour mixture and then a quarter of the milk mixture. Continue alternating between the two mixtures until they have both been completely added to the batter. Beat for a final 30 seconds to fully combine the batter (but make sure you do not overmix, as you may end up with a tough cake).

{CONTINUED}

BAKE THE CAKE Pour the cake batter into the prepared baking dish and spread it out evenly using a rubber spatula. Bake for 45 minutes, or until a skewer inserted into the center comes out clean. The top of the cake will be a deep golden brown.

Allow the cake to cool completely in the pan, about 30 minutes.

SOAK THE CAKE WITH THE MILKS Use a wooden skewer or other sharp, thin object to poke holes all over the top of the cake, including the edges and corners.

Combine the whole milk, sweetened condensed milk, and evaporated milk in a bowl and whisk well to fully incorporate the thick sweetened condensed milk into the mixture. Slowly pour the milk mixture over the cooled cake. It may seem as if the cake will not be able to absorb all of the liquid, but keep going—it will all soak in. Allow the cake to rest in the refrigerator while you prepare the meringue.

PREPARE THE MERINGUE Place the egg whites, sugar, and salt in the work bowl of a stand mixer or a metal mixing bowl and set over a pot of simmering water. Stir the egg white mixture until the sugar and salt are dissolved and the egg whites are warm to the touch, about 4 minutes. The mixture will be a bit frothy and milky in color.

Remove the bowl from the pot and beat on high speed (using the whisk attachment if you're using a stand mixer) until the egg whites are stiff and glossy, about 5 minutes.

FINISH THE CAKE While the meringue is still warm, use a rubber spatula to spread it all over the top of the cake. For a decorative touch, create peaks of meringue by tapping the flat side of the spatula all over the topping. If you like, finish by caramelizing the surface of the meringue with a kitchen torch.

COOKING NOTES

EQUIPMENT

Because the cake will not be removed from the baking pan, select one that you will be happy serving the cake from. I like to use a rectangular white ceramic oven-proof dish.

TECHNIQUES

Swiss meringue See page 184.

Caramelizing the meringue Caramelizing or browning meringue gives it a depth of flavor and an attractive appearance. This is best done with a kitchen torch, which can be purchased at a kitchenware store. Follow the manufacturer's instructions for turning on the torch. Hold it about 4 inches away from the meringue and wave it back and forth over the surface of the topping until you achieve streaks of caramel brown color all over. If you do not have a torch, you may wish to garnish with a dusting of cocoa powder or cinnamon.

ADVANCE PREPARATION

The cake is best prepared a day in advance and allowed to rest in the refrigerator. The time in the refrigerator will allow the cake to absorb the milk mixture and also stiffen a bit, so that it doesn't fall apart when you cut into it.

Cuban Cookout

Drink

Mojito {72}

Starters

Chorizo Sliders with Guava
Ketchup / *Fritas Cubanas* {75}

Platter of Shrimp with Garlicky Cuban
Mojo / *Fuente de Camarones al Ajillo* {77}

Main Courses

Grilled Mahi-Mahi with Mango Salsa /
Mahi a la Parilla con Salsa de Mango {81}

Cuban Grilled Pork / *Lechon Asado* {82}

Sides

Grilled Ripe Plantains / *Platanos
Maduros a la Parrilla* {85}

Rice Cooked in Black Beans /
Moros y Cristianos {86}

Avocado Salad / *Ensalada de Aquacate* {87}

Dessert

Butter Rum Cake with Lime Icing /
Panetela Borracha {88}

Leftovers

Grilled Cuban Sandwich /
Sandwich Cubano {90}

Cuban cuisine is a wonderful blend of Spanish, African, and Caribbean influences—the Spanish influence being perhaps the strongest, as Cuba was once a Spanish colony. Although the flavors of Cuban cooking are highly spiced with garlic and cumin, they're not fiery and hot chiles are seldom used. Pork is immensely popular on the island; it and other meats are often served shredded, pulled, pounded, or chopped to stretch the servings. Due to Cuba's tropical climate, fruits and tubers, especially yams, bananas, and plantains, are abundant and are used in both sweet and savory dishes. Characteristic ingredients of Cuban cuisine include garlic and onion; green peppers; cumin and oregano; citrus fruits; rice and beans; root vegetables; plantains; and avocados.

{MENU GAME PLAN}

One day in advance:

- Bake the cake and make the lime icing. Ice the cake, but wait to garnish it with mint. Cover loosely. Storage: room temperature
- Prepare the chorizo slider meat mixture. Storage: refrigerator

The night before:

- Marinate the pork. Storage: refrigerator
- Prepare garlicky mojo for the shrimp. Storage: refrigerator
- Marinate the onions for the avocado salad. Storage: refrigerator
- Shape the chorizo slider patties. Storage: refrigerator

On the morning of:

- Prepare rice and beans and leave covered in the pot. Storage: room temperature
- Prepare the mango salsa for the fish. Storage: room temperature
- Prepare the butter glaze for the plantains. Storage: room temperature; however, the glaze will get hard and will need to be reheated

- Fry the potato sticks. Place in an airtight container. Storage: room temperature
- Prepare the guava ketchup. Storage: room temperature

Two to three hours before:

- Depending on the size of your piece of pork, you may need to start grilling now (see page 82).
- Devein and butterfly the shrimp. Storage: refrigerator
- Boil the pork marinade and puree. Storage: room temperature

In the hour before (setup):

- Set up the mojito bar.
- Set up a tray with ingredients for the chorizo sliders (buns, ketchup, and potato sticks).
- Set out:
  Garlicky mojo
  Mango salsa

As your event unfolds:

- Grill your pork as dictated by cut and required cooking time (see page 82).
- Serve mojitos.
- Grill and assemble the chorizo sliders and serve them with the guava ketchup.
- Grill the shrimp and serve it with the garlicky mojo.
- Grill the plantains.
- Grill the fish.
- Finish the pork, pulling or shredding it by hand.
- Slice the avocados for the salad and serve with the marinated onions.
- Set out the Moros y Cristianos (beans and rice).
- Serve the main courses and sides.
- Garnish the cake with fresh mint.
- Serve dessert.
- Wrap and store leftover pork for Cuban Sandwiches.

MOJITO

Made famous by Ernest Hemingway, the mojito is considered by many to be Cuba's national cocktail. The drink gets its name from the African word *mojo*, which means "to cast a spell." Appropriate, considering how good just one mojito makes you feel! **Makes 1 cocktail**

¼ cup lightly packed fresh mint leaves
4 teaspoons sugar
½ lime, cut into 4 small pieces
Ice
2 ounces white rum
4 ounces club soda
Fresh mint sprig, for garnish
Stick of sugar cane, for garnish

MUDDLE THE MINT AND LIME Rip the mint leaves into small pieces by hand and place them in a tall glass. Add the sugar and lime pieces and muddle or mash the ingredients until all the juice has been squeezed out of the lime and the sugar has dissolved.

FINISH THE COCKTAIL Fill the glass with ice and then pour in the rum and club soda. Stir well and garnish with a mint sprig and/or a sugar cane stick.

COOKING NOTES

INGREDIENTS

Club soda Refrigerate your club soda so that it is chilled when added to the cocktail. This will prevent the ice from melting too quickly, helping the drink keep its fizz.

TECHNIQUE

Making mojitos for a group I have never made a pitcher of mojitos with success. The club soda tends to fizzle out, and it is impossible to evenly distribute the muddled lime and mint leaves. Instead of making a pitcher of mojitos, muddle a batch of mint, lime, and sugar (below are the measurements for six servings; this can easily be doubled).

To make a pitcher for 6:
1½ cups lightly packed fresh mint leaves
½ cup sugar
3 limes, each cut into 8 pieces
12 ounces white rum
24 ounces club soda

Divide the ingredients into glasses and top each with ice, rum, and club soda.

ADVANCE PREPARATION

The mint leaves, lime, and sugar can be muddled and kept for a couple of hours in an airtight container until ready to serve.

CHORIZO SLIDERS with Guava Ketchup
{FRITAS CUBANAS}

As legend has it, these highly seasoned burgers got their start in a Cuban sausage factory. In order to make sure the seasoning for the chorizo sausage was perfect, a small amount of the sausage filling was quickly fried up and tasted. Eventually, the samples became a popular midday snack. Because they pack a powerful punch of flavor, the patties are purposely made thin and small. You can think of these sliders as mini chorizo burger patties that are piled high with fried potato sticks. **Serves 12**

Slider Mix
1 tablespoon olive oil
1 clove garlic, peeled and crushed
½ small onion, chopped (about ½ cup)
1 tablespoon hot paprika
1 tablespoon smoked paprika
1 teaspoon ground cumin
2 teaspoons salt
¼ cup ketchup
1½ tablespoons Worcestershire sauce
¾ pound ground beef, preferably chuck
¼ pound ground pork

Potato Sticks
2 russet potatoes, unpeeled and cut into
    matchsticks or thin strips
Vegetable oil for frying
Salt

Guava Ketchup
¼ cup ketchup
¼ cup guava jelly
1½ teaspoons Worcestershire sauce
12 slider (miniature hamburger) buns, preferably
    potato bread

SAUTÉ THE ONION AND GARLIC Place the olive oil and garlic in a sauté pan set over medium-high heat. When the garlic begins to sizzle (about 45 seconds), add the onion and sauté until the onion becomes limp and translucent, about 3 minutes. Add both paprikas, cumin, and salt, and stir to combine.

PREPARE THE SLIDER MIX Place the onion and garlic mixture, ketchup, and Worcestershire sauce in a blender and puree until smooth. Place the beef and pork in a medium bowl and pour the puree over the meat. Using your hands, work the puree into the meat until well mixed. Allow the meat mixture to rest in the refrigerator for about 1 hour.

PREPARE THE POTATO STICKS Line a dish with paper towels and set aside. Pour 2 inches of oil into a deep, heavy-bottomed pot. Place the pot over high heat and wait for the oil to reach 375°F on a deep-fry thermometer. If you don't have a deep-fry thermometer, you can test the oil temperature by dropping a couple of potato sticks in the oil—if bubbles rise up around the potatoes, it's ready. Sprinkle a small amount (about a four-finger pinch) of the potato sticks into the hot oil (small batches keep the potatoes from forming into one large mass).

When the potatoes cook to a golden brown color, in about 2 minutes, remove them from the oil with a slotted spoon and place on the paper towel–lined dish to drain. Immediately season with salt. Repeat with the remaining potato sticks until all are cooked, drained, and salted. Some of the potato sticks will have stuck together. When they have cooled, gently break apart.

{CONTINUED}

PREPARE THE GUAVA KETCHUP In a small bowl, mix together the ketchup, guava jelly, and Worcestershire sauce until well combined.

SHAPE AND COOK THE PATTIES Heat your grill to high (550°F) and close the lid. Wait at least 15 minutes before lowering the heat to medium-high (450°F) and continuing. (Alternatively, you can use a griddle over medium-high heat.)

While the grill is heating, roll about ¼ cup of the meat mixture into a ball and lightly flatten into a patty about ½ inch thick. Repeat with the remaining mixture. Oil the grill grates with a vegetable oil–soaked paper towel held with a long pair of tongs. Cook the patties for about 3 minutes per side.

ASSEMBLE THE SLIDERS AND SERVE Slather the guava ketchup on both sides of a bun. Layer a mound of potato sticks on the bottom bun, place a patty over it, then top with another mound of potato sticks and the other half of the bun. Serve.

COOKING NOTES

INGREDIENTS

Potato sticks You can easily substitute store-bought potato chips or sticks for the homemade version. I recommend using the colorful root vegetable chips that come in stick form, or simply use your favorite bagged potato chip.

Hamburger buns Any type of miniature (slider-size) hamburger bun can be used; however, soft potato bread is the most authentic. If you cannot find slider-size buns, substitute split dinner rolls.

Guava ketchup The guava jelly adds sweetness to the ketchup. In the event you cannot find it, apricot jelly can be substituted.

TECHNIQUE

Grill versus griddle A *plancha,* or stovetop griddle, is traditionally used to cook these sliders. However, they can easily be grilled as well.

ADVANCE PREPARATION

The slider mix, potato sticks, and guava ketchup can all be made up to 2 days in advance. Keep the slider mix and ketchup in the refrigerator and store the potato sticks in an airtight container.

PLATTER OF SHRIMP with Garlicky Cuban Mojo
{FUENTE DE CAMARONES AL AJILLO}

Here I have taken a Cuban classic, *camarones al ajillo* (shrimp in garlic sauce), and adapted it for backyard entertaining. I was also inspired by the crowd-pleasing mounds of cold poached shrimp with sides of cocktail sauce you see at buffets. So I grilled jumbo shrimp, piled them on a platter, and served them with *mojo,* the addictively delicious citrus-garlic sauce that has become synonymous with Cuban cooking. **Serves 8**

Mojo
7 cloves garlic, peeled
2 teaspoons salt
⅓ cup lime juice (from 4 to 5 limes)
¼ cup orange juice (from 1 orange)
¼ cup olive oil

Shrimp
2 pounds jumbo shrimp, peeled, deveined, and
    butterflied
¼ cup vegetable oil
Salt and black pepper
2 limes, cut into small wedges

PREPARE THE MOJO Make a wet garlic paste by mashing the garlic cloves with salt in a mortar and pestle. If you do not have one, you can use a cup and the back of a wooden spoon; otherwise, simply sprinkle the garlic with the salt and use your knife to chop it very finely into a paste.

Place the garlic paste in a small bowl and pour the lime juice and orange juice over it. Allow the mixture to sit for 20 minutes.

Place the olive oil in a small saucepan and set it over medium-high heat. (This can be done on your grill or on your stove.) When small bubbles begin to rise to the surface of the oil, carefully add the garlic and citrus mixture to the pan (the oil will sizzle a bit, so be careful that it does not splatter on you). Give the mixture a quick stir and allow to cook over medium-high heat for 1 minute before removing from the heat. Set aside.

{CONTINUED}

COOKING NOTES

INGREDIENTS

Mojo Pronounced *MOH-hoh, mojo* is the condiment most often used in Cuban cooking—it can be used as a marinade or a dipping sauce. (Note that while the name of the sauce is similar to that of the mojito cocktail, the two concoctions have no other similarities.) Mojos are always oil-based and always contain citrus juice. This recipe is for the version used as a dipping sauce; those used for marinades contain ground cumin and/or dried oregano (see the recipe for Cuban Grilled Pork on page 82).

TECHNIQUE

Butterflied shrimp A butterflied shrimp has been evenly split lengthwise down its center and cut almost all the way through (note that sometimes it is cut all the way through, into two pieces). When opened, it has the shape of a butterfly. I like to use this technique on shrimp so that it cooks evenly and quickly (shrimp easily overcook and can turn tough and rubbery).

Place the tip of your knife blade in the indentation created on the shrimp's back by the deveining process. Slice the shrimp ¾ of the way through, so that the flesh is still connected on one side.

ADVANCE PREPARATION

The mojo can be made a day in advance and kept refrigerated. Heat over medium heat in a saucepan until warm before serving.

SEASON AND GRILL THE SHRIMP Place the shrimp in a large mixing bowl and drizzle the vegetable oil over them. Liberally season with salt and pepper and toss well. It's best to use your hands for this, as you want to make sure the oil and seasonings get inside the slits you made in the shrimp.

Heat your grill to high (550°F) and close the lid. Wait at least 15 minutes before lowering the heat to medium-high (450°F) and continuing. Oil the grill grates with a vegetable oil–soaked paper towel held with a long pair of tongs.

It is important to properly place the shrimp on the grill so that they cook quickly and evenly.

Again, its best to use your hands for this. Holding the shrimp by its tail, place the butterflied shrimp on the grill one by one, slit side down. Curl the tail down towards the head of the shrimp. Close the lid and cook for about 5 minutes, or until the flesh of the shrimp has turned white and is no longer translucent. You will not need to turn the shrimp over.

SERVE THE SHRIMP AND MOJO Mound the grilled shrimp on a large platter and garnish with lime wedges. Serve with the garlicky mojo for your guests to use as a dipping sauce.

GRILLED MAHI-MAHI with Mango Salsa
{MAHI A LA PARRILLA CON SALSA DE MANGO}

Simply grilled fish brightened with a squeeze of fresh lime is a very typical Cuban dish. Snacking on fresh mango is also very popular on the island. Combining the two, however, was a Miami invention that many have come to really enjoy. A light and refreshing alternative to beef on the grill, this is the fish recipe I make the most—and I never get tired of it! **Serves 8**

Mango Salsa
2 ripe mangoes, peeled and chopped
½ small red onion, finely chopped (about ½ cup)
1 jalapeño chile, stemmed and finely chopped
¼ cup lightly packed cilantro leaves and tender
    stems, finely chopped, plus more sprigs for
    garnish
¼ cup lime juice (from 3 limes)
½ teaspoon salt
Black pepper

8 mahi-mahi fillets (about 4 pounds total)
4 limes
1 cup olive oil
Salt and black pepper

PREPARE THE MANGO SALSA Place all the salsa ingredients in a mixing bowl and toss to combine. Allow to sit for at least 15 minutes at room temperature while you prepare the fish.

PREPARE THE GRILL AND SEASON THE FISH Heat your grill to medium-high (450°F) and close the lid. Wait at least 15 minutes before continuing. Oil the grill grates with a vegetable oil–soaked paper towel held with a long pair of tongs.

Squeeze half a lime and drizzle 2 teaspoons of olive oil over each fillet (get the juice and oil on both sides) and then season with salt and pepper.

GRILL THE FISH AND SERVE Place the fish on the grill and close the lid. Grill the fish for 8 minutes, or until you see grill marks and the bottom half of the flesh becomes opaque. Flip and cook for another 6 to 8 minutes. The fish is ready when the bottom half of the flesh has become opaque and the top flesh begins to flake.

COOKING NOTES

INGREDIENTS

Mahi-Mahi Mahi-mahi is a firm and flavorful fish that has a moderate amount of fat, making it a good grilling fish. It is also known as dolphin fish, but its Hawaiian name, mahi-mahi, is more commonly used.

If you cannot find mahi-mahi, you can substitute grouper, tilapia, or halibut in this recipe.

TECHNIQUES

Successfully grilling fish Fish is tricky to cook well on a grill. For starters, it tends to dry out quickly; but probably most frustrating is that it tends to stick to the grates even when they are well oiled. My approach is to use dense and meaty fish rather than flaky fish. I've listed some suggestions above in the Ingredients note above, but when in doubt, look for steak cuts or thick, dense fillets.

Chopping a mango Peel the mango first, using a vegetable peeler or a small paring knife. Mangoes have a single large seed in the center that you will need to cut around. It may take a bit of trial and error to remove as much flesh from around the seed as possible. After you have removed the flesh, chop it.

ADVANCE PREPARATION

The mango salsa can be made a few hours before serving and stored at room temperature.

Place the fish on a platter. Top each fillet with a spoonful of salsa and garnish with sprigs of cilantro. Serve any remaining salsa on the side.

CUBAN GRILLED PORK {LECHON ASADO}

Cubans love their pork. It's hard to find a Cuban or Cuban-American who doesn't have a memory of spending hours waiting for a *lechon* to finish cooking in someone's backyard, and then sharing it with family and friends (I am certainly no exception). What sets Cuban-style pork apart is the use of *mojo criollo*, a highly seasoned marinade made up of tangy citrus juice, vast amounts of garlic, cumin, and oregano. And while roasting a whole pig is deliciously fun, smaller cuts are far more manageable and easier to work with. So I've come up with a chart outlining various cuts and their cooking times, and the approximate amount of marinade you will need to begin making your own memories.

Citrus Garlic Marinade (see chart for amounts
    per cut)
Pork (see chart for cut and size)
Salt

PREPARE THE MARINADE Mix all marinade ingredients in a bowl and let sit for 10 minutes.

MARINATE THE PORK If using a flavor injector (see Cooking Notes), strain half the marinade into a bowl, adding the strained-out garlic to the other half of the marinade. Use the injector to take in some strained marinade, pierce the pork with the tip of the needle, and inject it into the flesh. Do this all over the meat until the strained marinade has been used up.

If you are not using a flavor injector, use a long, thin knife to create deep gashes all over the flesh and pour the marinade over the pork.

Place the marinated pork in a deep bowl or container. Generously season the outside of the pork with salt and pour the remaining marinade all over it, spreading the onion rings all over the top.

Cover well with plastic wrap and refrigerate for at least 1 hour or up to 24 hours.

BOIL THE MARINADE FOR BASTING (This does not apply when you're preparing a whole pig.) Remove the pork from the marinade and place it on a platter. Transfer the marinade to a saucepan, add the onions, and bring to a boil for 2 minutes. Remove from the heat and allow to cool. Place the boiled marinade and onions in a blender and puree until smooth. The marinade is now ready to use as a basting liquid.

GRILL THE PORK Before heating your grill, remove the pork from the refrigerator and bring to room temperature. Depending on the size of the cut this could take 15 minutes (small pork tenderloin) to 1 hour (a larger leg).

Heat your grill to high (550°F) and close the lid. Wait at least 15 minutes before lowering the heat to the temperature required for the cut you are using. Oil the grill grates with a vegetable oil–soaked paper towel held with a long pair of tongs.

If your cut has the skin still attached, begin the cooking process with the skin side up (away from the direct heat).

Grill your meat according to the time outlined in the chart. Turn the meat over once when you are one quarter through with the cooking time, again when you are halfway through, and once more when three-quarters of the cooking time has elapsed. The pork is ready when it reaches an internal temperature of 150°F on the grill (it will continue to cook when it's off the heat, raising the internal temperature to the desired 160°F).

{CONTINUED ON PAGE 84}

Cooking Times Guide

	Whole Pig	Leg (fresh ham)	Shoulder butt (blade roast)	Loin	Tenderloin
Size/Weight	45 pounds	15 to 20 pounds	6 to 8 pounds	3 pounds	1 pound
Serves	40 to 50	20 to 30	10 to 12	4 to 6	2 to 4
Marinade Quantity	13½ cups (triple the recipe)	9 cups (double the recipe)	4½ cups (1 recipe)	2¼ cups (half of the recipe)	1 cup (one quarter of the recipe)
Grill Temperature	Low (300°F)	Low (300°F)	Low (300°F)	Medium (400°F)	Medium-high (450°F)
Approximate Cooking Time	6 to 7 hours	4 hours	2½ hours	45 to 60 minutes	16 to 20 minutes

Citrus Garlic Marinade

Marinade Ingredients	Whole Pig (triple recipe)	Leg (fresh ham) (double recipe)	Shoulder butt (blade roast) (1 recipe)	Loin (half of the recipe)	Tenderloin (one quarter of the recipe)
Seville orange juice	12 cups (3 quarts)	8 cups (2 quarts)	4 cups (1 quart)	2 cups	1 cup
or Lime juice and Orange juice	8 cups 4 cups	5⅓ cups 2⅔ cups	2⅔ cups 1⅓ cup	1⅓ cup ⅔ cup	⅔ cup ⅓ cup
Ground cumin	3 tablespoons	2 tablespoons	1 tablespoon	1½ teaspoon	¾ teaspoon
Dried oregano	6 tablespoons	¼ cup	2 tablespoons	1 tablespoon	1½ teaspoons
Garlic	6 heads	4 heads	2 heads	1 head	8 cloves
Salt	½ cup plus 1 tablespoon	6 tablespoons	3 tablespoons	4½ teaspoons	2¼ teaspoons
Black pepper	3 tablespoons	2 tablespoons	1 tablespoon	1½ teaspoons	¾ teaspoon
Onion	None	4	2	1	½

COOKING NOTES

INGREDIENTS

Seville oranges A Seville orange is a bitter orange that is sometimes referred to as a sour orange. Its thick skin is pale yellow and its flesh contains many seeds. Due to its very sour taste, it is not an eating orange. In the event you cannot find Seville oranges, substitute a 2:1 ratio of lime juice and regular orange juice.

TECHNIQUES

Flavor injector Cuban-style pork is very well seasoned both inside and out. A flavor injector, a kitchen tool that resembles a needle and syringe, is used to marinate the interior flesh of thick cuts of pork. If you do not have one, simply make deep gashes with a thin knife all over the meat and pour the marinade over and into the cuts. Thinner cuts such as the loin and tenderloin do not require a flavor injector, but they should still be pierced with a knife before being coated with marinade.

Injecting the flesh To prevent the garlic from getting stuck in the injector tip, strain half of the marinade and use that in the injector.

When you inject the marinade into the pork, you will see a bulge appear close to the site of the injection. That is the marinade settling into the flesh. When the pork is cooked, you may see pockets of darker flesh in the areas where the marinade was injected; this is normal.

Freezing citrus juice Because I use so much citrus juice in my cooking and insist on using only juice from fresh fruit, I always freeze leftover juice from recipes or from fruit that is just about to go bad for future use. If placed in an airtight container, citrus juice will keep for a few months. Simply thaw at room temperature before using.

ADVANCE PREPARATION

The marinade can be made a day in advance. All cuts can be left marinating for 24 hours.

GRILLED RIPE PLANTAINS
{PLÁTANOS MADUROS A LA PARRILLA}

Plantains, ripe or unripe, are a staple of Cuban cooking. And while everyone loves the ripe ones (*maduros*), no one ever wants to make them. Typically deep-fried, they are a mess to make and never seem to come out with that candylike coating you get at good restaurants. This recipe solves the problem: simply grilling very ripe plantains and basting them with a butter-sugar glaze is all it takes to re-create the good stuff. These are a must at all my family cookouts. **Serves 8**

3 tablespoons unsalted butter
¾ cup packed brown sugar
2 tablespoons apple cider vinegar or sherry
    vinegar
4 very ripe (black) plantains

PREPARE THE BUTTER GLAZE Place the butter and sugar in a small saucepan over medium heat and cook until the butter is melted and the sugar is dissolved in it. Add the vinegar and stir well. Remove from the heat and set aside.

PREPARE, GRILL, AND SERVE THE PLANTAINS
Heat your grill to high (550°F) and close the lid. Wait at least 15 minutes before lowering the heat to medium-high (450°F) and continuing. Oil the grill grates with a vegetable oil–soaked paper towel held with a long pair of tongs.

COOKING NOTES

INGREDIENTS
    Plantains See page 66.

ADVANCE PREPARATION
    You can prepare the butter glaze a few hours in advance. It will thicken when cool and will need to be reheated.

Slice the unpeeled plantains in half lengthwise and place them cut side down on the grill. Close the lid and cook for 15 minutes. Turn the plantains over and baste the cut sides of the plantains with the butter glaze. Close the lid and continue cooking for another 15 minutes. Brush a bit more glaze on the plantains before removing them from the grill.

Serve the plantains in their skins while hot from the grill.

The Three Stages of a Plantain

Type	Unripe Plantain/ *Plátano Verde*	Yellow Plantain/ *Plátano Pintón*	Ripe Plantain/ *Plátano Maduro*
Composition	Very high starch; low sugar	Moderate starch; moderate sugar	Low starch; high sugar
Best Cooking Method	Fried	Boiled (usually mashed)	Grilled, fried, or roasted
Best Seasoning	Salt and lime	Onion, garlic, pork cracklings	Sugar, butter

RICE COOKED IN BLACK BEANS
{MOROS Y CRISTIANOS}

This dish gets its name from the wars between the dark-skinned Moors (*moros*) and the light-skinned Spaniards (*cristianos*) that occurred during the eighth century in Spain. It's a very popular Cuban dish, and it's perfect for outdoor entertaining, as it can be made well in advance and be served at room temperature. **Serves 8 to 10**

4 cloves garlic, peeled
3 teaspoons salt
¼ pound bacon (about 6 strips), chopped
2 tablespoons olive oil
1 onion, finely chopped (about 1 cup)
1 green pepper, seeded and finely chopped
    (about ¾ cup)
1 bay leaf
¼ teaspoon ground cumin
½ teaspoon dried oregano
1½ cups long-grain white rice
2 (15½-ounce) cans black beans, not drained
1¾ cups water
1 tablespoon red wine vinegar

MASH THE GARLIC AND RENDER THE BACON FAT
Put the garlic on a cutting board and sprinkle 1 teaspoon of salt over the cloves, let it sit for a few minutes, and mince it into a paste with a knife. Set aside.

Place the bacon and olive oil in a large pot and set it over medium-high heat. Sauté the bacon until it renders its fat and turns a golden brown color, about 6 minutes. Move the bacon around as it's cooking to prevent it from sticking to the bottom of the pot.

SAUTÉ THE VEGETABLES AND RICE Add the onion, green pepper, and garlic paste to the bacon and sauté until the vegetables are limp and translucent, about 5 minutes. Add the remaining 2 teaspoons of salt, the bay leaf, cumin, oregano, and rice and stir for 1 minute until well mixed and all the rice is coated in oil.

COOKING NOTES

INGREDIENTS

Canned black beans If you do not want to use the liquid from the canned black beans, just add an extra ½ cup of water with the drained and rinsed black beans.

TECHNIQUE

Cooking the rice Rice requires a specific amount of liquid to cook properly. Because onions and green peppers can contribute a considerable amount of liquid to a recipe, a volume measure for each is given. While the measurements are approximate, making sure the chopped vegetables are close to these amounts will ensure that the rice cooks properly.

ADVANCE PREPARATION

You can prepare the recipe in its entirety the night before with very little effect on the taste and texture of the dish. However, you will want to warm the dish before serving. This can be done in the microwave or on the stovetop. Just sprinkle about ¼ cup of water over the rice to make sure it does not dry out when reheated.

ADD THE BEANS, SIMMER, AND SERVE Add the beans and their liquid, along with the water and vinegar, to the pot. Cover and bring to a boil, then reduce to a simmer. Cook for 35 to 40 minutes, or until all the water has been absorbed by the rice. Allow the covered pot to sit off the heat for 5 minutes. Fluff the rice with a fork and serve.

AVOCADO SALAD {ENSALADA DE AGUACATE}

Salad greens are hard to come by in Cuban cooking. But an avocado salad—simply made by topping sliced avocado with red onion slices, olive oil, and vinegar—is both traditional and refreshing. Serves 6 to 8

½ red onion, thinly sliced
1 cup red wine vinegar
1 Florida avocado or 2 Hass avocados
    (about 1 pound total), sliced
1 tablespoon highest-quality extra-virgin olive oil
Salt and black pepper

MARINATE THE ONION Place the onion slices and vinegar in a resealable plastic bag, press out as much air as possible, and close the bag. Alternatively, place the onion and vinegar in a small bowl and put a piece of plastic wrap directly on the surface of the ingredients so that the onion slices remain submerged in the vinegar. Allow the onion to marinate for at least 30 minutes.

ASSEMBLE THE SALAD AND SERVE Reserve a few tablespoons of the vinegar used to marinate the onion before draining the onion slices and setting aside. Place the avocado slices on a serving platter and top with the red onion slices. Drizzle the oil and reserved red wine vinegar over the salad and season with salt and pepper to taste.

--- COOKING NOTES ---

INGREDIENTS

Florida versus Hass Avocados Cubans tend to use Florida avocados since these are more widely available in the Caribbean and in Miami. They are larger than the California or Hass variety, and they remain green when ripe, in contrast to Hass, which are dark green, almost black, when ripe.

Florida avocados have a milder flavor due to their higher water content, and they are ready to eat as soon as they yield to pressure when squeezed lightly.

TECHNIQUES

Marinating onions Allowing raw onions to marinate in vinegar or another highly acidic liquid mellows out the strong flavor and softens its texture.

Slicing an avocado See page 46.

ADVANCE PREPARATION

The onions can be left marinating up to a few days in advance. However, while the oil and vinegar help slow down the browning of the avocado's flesh, it's best to slice the avocado shortly before serving.

BUTTER RUM CAKE with Lime Icing
{PANETELA BORRACHA}

Rum cake has always been a Cuban staple at weddings, birthdays, Christmas parties, and celebrations of all kinds. The secret ingredient in this recipe is the package of instant pudding mix added to the cake batter—it makes the cake perfectly moist every time. Another feature of this recipe is the touch of lime juice I add to the icing, and the mint garnish—it's my ode to the mojito cocktail. Serves 12 to 18

Cake Batter
2 sticks (1 cup) unsalted butter, at room
    temperature
1½ cups sugar
4 eggs
2 cups cake flour
2 teaspoons baking powder
1 teaspoon salt
1 (3½-ounce) package vanilla instant
    pudding mix
½ cup milk
½ cup light rum
1 teaspoon vanilla extract

Rum Syrup
½ stick (¼ cup) butter
1 cup sugar
¼ cup water
¼ cup light rum

Lime Icing
Juice of 1 lime (about 1 tablespoon)
¾ cup confectioners' sugar
1 bunch fresh mint

PREPARE THE BATTER AND BAKE THE CAKE Preheat the oven to 350°F. Grease and flour a 12-cup Bundt pan. Set aside.

Using a handheld electric mixer or stand mixer with the paddle attachment, beat the butter and sugar until well combined and the mixture is pale yellow and fluffy, 2 to 4 minutes depending on your mixer. Add the eggs and continue beating until the mixture is light and fluffy, about 3 minutes. Scrape the bottom and sides of the bowl with a rubber spatula if necessary.

Combine the flour, baking powder, salt, and vanilla pudding mix in a bowl and set aside. Combine the milk, rum, and vanilla in a measuring cup and set aside.

Alternate adding the flour mixture and the milk mixture to the butter and eggs, mixing until all the ingredients are well incorporated. Pour the cake batter into the prepared Bundt pan and bake for 1 hour. The cake is ready when a skewer inserted in the center comes out clean. You may also see the sides of the cake shrink away from the pan.

SYRUP AND SOAK THE CAKE

ugar, and water in a pan and sim-
id becomes slightly thickened,
The mixture will foam a bit. Stir
lower the heat if the mixture
over. When the mixture has thick-
m and stir well. Remove from the
le.

As soon as you remove the cake from the oven,
poke holes all over its surface with a long skewer.
Slowly drizzle all of the rum syrup over the cake (it
may seem like overkill, but make sure you use all the
syrup). Allow the cake to cool completely in the pan.
Once the cake is cool, invert it onto a serving dish.

PREPARE THE LIME ICING AND ICE THE CAKE Mix
the lime juice and confectioners' sugar in a small
bowl until the sugar is dissolved. It should be the
consistency of mayonnaise. Drizzle or pipe the
icing over the top of the cake, allowing it to drip
down the sides. Garnish by placing plenty of fresh
mint sprigs in the center hole of the cake.

COOKING NOTES

TECHNIQUES

Piping the lime icing In order to drizzle the
icing properly, you can carefully pour it over
the cake, allowing it to drip down the sides.
Alternatively, you can create a piping bag with
a resealable plastic bag. Pour the icing into the
plastic bag and push it toward a bottom corner.
Snip off the tip and pipe the icing through.

Bundt pan I like using a Bundt pan for a
couple of reasons: it allows for easy slicing and
serving, and its center hole is perfect for holding
the bunch of fresh mint.

ADVANCE PREPARATION

The rum glaze can be made while you're waiting for the cake to bake. After all the ingredients
have been combined, set it aside in the pan, off
the heat, then gently warm it before drizzling it
over the cake.

The mint should not be placed on the cake
until it is ready to be served, as it will quickly wilt
at room temperature.

GRILLED CUBAN SANDWICH
{SANDWICH CUBANO}

As soon as someone finds out about my Cuban background, a Cuban sandwich question is never far away. It's no wonder, since Cuban sandwiches have recently popped up on menus all over the country. While many have gotten close to re-creating the real thing, I feel most miss the mark. So here is a step-by-step guide to creating an authentic *sandwich Cubano*. This is also a great way to use up the leftovers from your Cuban pig roast! **Serves 8**

1 loaf Cuban bread, sliced lengthwise
½ stick (¼ cup) unsalted butter, softened
3 tablespoons yellow mustard, or to taste
1½ pounds boiled ham, sliced
1½ pounds roasted pork, sliced
1 pound Swiss cheese, sliced
1 cup dill pickle chips, or to taste

ASSEMBLE THE SANDWICH Spread 2 tablespoons of the butter on one half of the bread loaf and a thin layer of mustard on the other. Place 1 to 2 layers of ham, pork, cheese, and, finally, pickles on the buttered bread and top with the mustard-spread bread.

WRAP THE SANDWICH IN FOIL Smear the remaining butter all over the outside of the sandwich and wrap it completely in aluminum foil.

PRESS AND GRILL THE SANDWICH Heat your grill to high (550°F) and close the lid. Wait at least 15 minutes before lowering the heat to medium-high (450°F) and continuing.

Before grilling the sandwich, press down on it with your hands to flatten it. Place the wrapped, flattened sandwich on the grill and top with a brick, grill press, or any other heavy, heat-resistant object. Close the lid and grill for 5 to 6 minutes per side.

Remove the wrapped sandwich from the grill and take off the foil. Return the sandwich to the grill and grill for about 2 to 3 minutes per side, or until both pieces of bread are crispy and golden brown.

SLICE AND SERVE Remove the sandwich from the grill and cut at an angle into small sandwich wedges (triangles). Place on a large platter and serve while still hot.

COOKING NOTES

INGREDIENTS

Cuban bread Made from white flour, yeast, and a bit of lard, this bread has a very thin crust and soft middle filled with tunnels. Cuban bread is distinguished by the palm frond placed lengthwise down its middle prior to baking, its length (almost 3 feet), and its somewhat rectangular shape.

ADVANCE PREPARATION

The loaf sandwich can be prepared and wrapped in foil a few hours in advance. Press and grill right before serving.

VARIATION: MEDIANOCHE SANDWICH

As an alternative to the Cuban sandwich try a *medianoche* (midnight) sandwich, which has the exact same fillings but is made with a sweet egg bread, which is referred to as *pan de medianoche*, or midnight sandwich bread. These golden brown hoagie-shaped breads can be found at most Latin markets, or you can substitute challah or brioche.

THE BUILDING BLOCKS OF A CUBAN SANDWICH ARE:

- A thin layer of yellow mustard on the top piece of bread
- A single layer of dill pickle chips
- A few slices of Swiss cheese
- 1 to 2 layers of roast pork
- 1 to 2 layers of sweet boiled ham
- A thin layer of softened butter on the bottom piece of bread

KEEP IN MIND:

1. Cuban bread makes a Cuban sandwich. If you can't find Cuban bread, good alternatives are ciabatta or panini bread, since they have a similar soft, airy middle.
2. The sandwich must be pressed.
3. The fillings must be warm, the cheese melted, and the bread toasted.
4. The mustard has to be simple yellow American mustard.
5. Dill pickle chips must be included.

Northern Andean Barbecue

Drink
Cold Venezuelan Beer

Starter
Cornmeal-Cheese Pancakes / *Arepas* {94}

Main Courses
Salt-Crusted Beef Tenderloin Charred in Cloth / *Lomo al Trapo* {95}

Brown Sugar–Crusted Grilled Chicken / *Pollo Asado Negro* {98}

Condiments & Sides
Fresh Tomato Salsa / *Salsa Pica* {99}

Tangy Avocado Sauce / *Salsa Guasca* {100}

Coconut Rice / *Arroz con Coco* {101}

Dessert
Venezuelan Chocolate Pudding with Espresso Cream {102}

Northern Andean food (the cooking of Colombia and Venezuela) blends African and indigenous cuisines with a scattering of European traditions brought by immigrants. These countries' highly diverse populations and topography have shaped a varied cuisine that differs greatly from region to region, as seen in the Caribbean-influenced coasts of Colombia and Venezuela, the indigenous traditions found in the mountain cities of Colombia, and the sophisticated European impact felt in the valley capital of Venezuela. Chocolate and coffee are essential flavors here. Venezuela is an important producer of premium cacao: though the country produces less than 1 percent of the world's cacao beans, they are some of the best in the world. And Colombia is a major producer of the highly regarded Arabica coffee bean. Other key ingredients of the northern Andes include plantains, rice, white farmer's cheese, corn, and beef. Although Venezuela may not be known for its beer, Venezuelans love it and favor light pilsner-style beer. In fact, Venezuela has the highest per capita beer consumption in Latin America.

{MENU GAME PLAN}

One day in advance:
- Prepare the chocolate pudding. Storage: refrigerator

The night before:
- Prepare and shape the Arepas. Storage: refrigerator
- Marinate the chicken. Storage: refrigerator

On the morning of:
- Prepare the Tangy Avocado Sauce. Storage: refrigerator

Two to three hours before:
- Prepare the Coconut Rice and leave it in the pot. Storage: room temperature
- Toast the coconut flakes. Storage: room temperature
- Prepare the espresso cream and place it in a resealable plastic bag. Storage: refrigerator

- Prepare the Fresh Tomato Salsa; however, do not add the salt until ready to serve. Cover with a damp towel. Storage: room temperature
- Prepare the tomatoes and onions for the chicken. Storage: room temperature

In the hour before (setup):
- Make sure the beer is cold. Set up the beverage bar.
- Place the rice, still in its covered pot, in a low (180°F) oven.
- Set up the ingredients for the Salt-Crusted Beef Tenderloin Charred in Cloth.
- Set out:
  Tangy Avocado Sauce
  Fresh Tomato Salsa

As your event unfolds:
- Grill the Arepas and serve as a starter.
- Grill the chicken.
- Prepare the salt-crusted beef packet.
- Grill the beef.
- Grill the onions and tomatoes.
- Season the Fresh Tomato Salsa with salt and set it out.
- Top the Coconut Rice with toasted coconut flakes and set it out.
- Carve the beef.
- Serve the main courses and sides.
- Pipe espresso cream onto the chocolate pudding.
- Serve dessert.

CORNMEAL-CHEESE PANCAKES {AREPAS}

Arepas are to Colombians and Venezuelans what tamales are to Mexicans: a popular corn-based snack eaten both at home and from street carts. These cakes are made with white cornmeal, fresh corn, and mild white cheese and griddled until hot and bubbly. The flavors are sweet and savory at the same time and go amazingly well with grilled meats. The white cornmeal used to make arepas isn't difficult to obtain (see below), so don't be discouraged; don't just substitute regular cornmeal—it won't work. I use mozzarella cheese in place of the traditional *queso telita*, or fresh farmer's cheese, which is more difficult to obtain. **Serves 8 to 10 (about sixteen 3-inch arepas)**

4½ cups (32 ounces) frozen corn, thawed
1½ cups precooked finely ground white cornmeal
½ pound mozzarella cheese, shredded (about
    2 cups)
1 teaspoon baking powder
½ cup milk
2 teaspoons salt

PREPARE THE CORN BATTER Puree the corn in a blender or food processor until just smooth. Transfer the puree to a large mixing bowl. Add the cornmeal, cheese, baking powder, milk, and salt to the bowl and stir until well combined. The mixture will be a bit wet and chunky. Allow the batter to sit for 5 minutes or until it thickens up a bit and you can easily form patties.

FORM THE PATTIES AND REFRIGERATE Take about ⅓ cup of the batter and roll it into a ball using your hands. Repeat with the remaining batter, making all the balls about the same size. Flatten each ball between the palms of your hands as you would a hamburger (the patties should be about 3 inches across and 2 inches thick). Place the formed patties on a sheet pan lined with parchment paper. Cover the pan with plastic wrap and refrigerate for 30 minutes.

GRILL THE AREPAS Place a grill topper on the grill grates. Heat your grill to high (550°F) and close the lid. Wait at least 15 minutes before lowering the heat to medium (400°F) and continuing. Brush vegetable oil all over the grill topper.

COOKING NOTES

INGREDIENTS

Harina P.A.N. This brand of the special cornmeal needed to make arepas has become so popular that it's synonymous with the actual ingredient. This finely ground precooked white cornmeal, which can be found in Latin markets and online, is not the same as the cornmeal used in Italian cooking.

EQUIPMENT

Grill toppers Grill toppers (also called grill sheets) offer a fantastic solution for grilling items that would otherwise stick to or fall through the grates. They are thin perforated metal sheets that sit directly on the grill grates.

ADVANCE PREPARATION

The arepas can be prepared and shaped a day in advance and kept refrigerated until you are ready to grill them.

Place the arepas on the grill topper and cook for 3 to 4 minutes per side. The arepas are ready when they turn a golden color and the cheese begins to ooze out of the top or sides.

SERVE Arepas are best eaten when still hot. Cut 8-inch squares of parchment paper to wrap around each cake so your guests can eat them with their hands.

SALT-CRUSTED BEEF TENDERLOIN Charred in Cloth
{LOMO AL TRAPO}

This has got to be one of the coolest recipes I know. The techniques used are so counterintuitive that you can't believe it actually works. The process is simple: cover the beef in an alarmingly large amount of salt, wrap it in a cotton kitchen towel, and then set it to burn on the grill. Your guests will think you have lost your mind until you unravel the mummified cloth and slice up the most tender, perfectly seasoned beef they will ever eat. **Serves 8**

3 pounds beef tenderloin, trimmed of all fat and
   silver skin
4 cups kosher salt

PREPARE THE GRILL Heat your grill to the highest setting and close the lid. Wait at least 15 minutes before continuing.

PREPARE THE MEAT Do this right before you are ready to start grilling. You will need a clean cotton kitchen towel and some cotton kitchen twine.

Lay the kitchen towel flat on a work surface. Spread about 1½ cups of salt in a line down the middle (if your tenderloin is as long as the towel, or nearly so, form the line diagonally). Set the tenderloin on the salt line and pour the rest of the salt over the beef (it will seem like overkill, but don't

worry). Fold the ends of the cloth over the ends of the beef and then fold the longer sides of the cloth over, completely covering the meat. Tie kitchen twine around the covered meat, securing the cloth so that it cannot unravel.

GRILL THE MEAT Place the bundled meat on the grill, lower the lid, and cook for 9 minutes. After a few minutes you will see smoke and smell the cotton towel burning. Leave it alone.

Carefully flip the bundled meat over and close the lid. Part of the cloth will be charred and may break off, which is fine. Close the grill lid and allow the meat to continue cooking for another 9 minutes. Check for doneness: Since you will not be able

{CONTINUED}

to see the meat, use an instant-read thermometer to check the doneness. Remove the meat when it reaches 5°F below your desired level (see page 10).

REMOVE THE CLOTH AND SERVE When the meat is removed from the grill, the cloth surrounding it will look charred and petrified. Allow the meat to rest for 5 minutes, then remove the cloth and scrape off the salt. Place the beef on a cutting board, slice the meat crosswise in ½-inch pieces, and serve.

--- COOKING NOTES ---

EQUIPMENT

Cloth and twine It is important that both the cloth and twine used be 100 percent cotton. Otherwise, they will go up in flames.

The cloth will still smolder and char, and it's the smoke produced by this charring that will infuse and flavor the beef.

ADVANCE PREPARATION

While you can have the meat and salt premeasured and the towel and twine ready to go, the bundle needs to be assembled right before you grill. Otherwise, the salt will draw out the moisture from the beef and you will end up with a tough piece of meat.

BROWN SUGAR–CRUSTED GRILLED CHICKEN
{POLLO ASADO NEGRO}

This recipe is an adaptation of a classic Venezuelan dish called *asado negro* (black roast), in which beef is slowly roasted in brown sugar until it is so caramelized that it turns black. The most intriguing part of the dish, to me, is the surprisingly balanced flavor combination—the sweetness of the sugar, the saltiness of the Worcestershire, and the punch of the garlic. Reworked to use chicken instead of beef, it's a great concept for the grill, as the brown sugar melts to form a delicious glaze that also serves to keep the chicken moist. **Serves 8**

7 cloves garlic, peeled and crushed
Salt
1¼ cups packed brown sugar
3 tablespoons Worcestershire sauce
2 tablespoons vegetable oil
Black pepper
2 pounds skin-on, bone-in chicken breasts
2 pounds skin-on, bone-in chicken legs
   and thighs
2 onions, cut into thick slices
2 tomatoes, cut into thick wedges
3 limes, cut into wedges

CREATE A GARLIC PASTE Place the crushed garlic cloves on your cutting board and sprinkle 1 teaspoon of salt over them. Wait a minute or so; you will notice moisture leaching from the garlic. Holding your knife blade almost parallel to the cutting board, scrape the blade over the chopped garlic. Repeat this motion a few times, until the garlic has turned into a semisoft paste. (Alternatively, use a mortar and pestle.) Set aside.

MARINATE THE CHICKEN In a large mixing bowl, combine the garlic paste, brown sugar, Worcestershire sauce, vegetable oil, and ½ teaspoon of black pepper. Stir until the sugar has dissolved. Add the chicken and toss until well coated with marinade. Cover and refrigerate for at least 30 minutes, or overnight.

COOKING NOTES

TECHNIQUE
   Why create a garlic paste? It helps prevent the garlic from burning on the grill and becoming bitter.

ADVANCE PREPARATION
   The chicken can be left marinating overnight.

GRILL THE VEGETABLES Place a grill topper on the grill grates. Heat your grill to high (550°F) and close the lid. Wait at least 15 minutes before lowering the heat to medium-high (450°F) and continuing.

Oil the grill topper with a vegetable oil–soaked paper towel held with a long pair of tongs. Place the onion slices on the topper, season with salt and pepper, and close the lid. Cook for 7 minutes, or until the onions develop a nice char on the bottom and begin to turn limp. Turn the onions over and add the tomatoes to the grill, skin side down; season both vegetables. Close the lid again and grill for an additional 5 minutes, or until the onions and tomatoes turn limp. Remove the vegetables and grill topper from the grill and place the onions and tomatoes on a serving platter.

GRILL THE CHICKEN Increase the grill heat to high (550°F), close the lid, and wait 15 minutes before continuing.

Oil the grill grates with a vegetable oil–soaked paper towel held with a long pair of tongs. Place the chicken breasts, skin side down, on the grill. With the heat on high and the lid open, grill for 10 minutes to crisp the skin and render some fat. Lower the heat to medium-high (450°F), turn the chicken over, add the chicken thighs and legs, and close the lid. Cook for an additional 10 minutes before flipping the chicken a final time. Cook for 10 more minutes, or until the chicken registers 160°F (it will continue to cook off the heat until it reaches the desired 165°F). Remove from the grill and place on the platter with the onion and tomatoes.

SERVE Garnish the platter of chicken, onions, and tomatoes with lime wedges and serve.

FRESH TOMATO SALSA {SALSA PICA}

Part sauce, part tomato salad, *salsa pica* is always found at Colombian cookouts. Some of my Colombian friends have told me the sauce gets it name from how it is prepared: it is *picado*, or chopped; others tell me its name comes from its spicy—*picante*—aspect. Whatever the case, its vibrant flavors and freshness make it the perfect complement to grilled meats. **Makes 2 cups**

2 large tomatoes, coarsely chopped
½ red onion, sliced thin
½ cup lightly packed cilantro leaves and tender
    stems, finely chopped
2 limes
Hot sauce
Salt

COMBINE ALL THE INGREDIENTS AND SERVE Place the tomatoes, onion, and cilantro in a bowl and toss to combine. Add the juice of the 2 limes and season with hot sauce and salt to taste. Serve.

COOKING NOTES

INGREDIENTS

Tomatoes Although round red tomatoes are typically used in salsa pica, try substituting yellow, orange, or other heirloom tomatoes when in season.

ADVANCE PREPARATION

You can prepare the salsa a few hours in advance so long as you hold off on adding the salt until right before serving. The salt will cause the vegetables to wilt and turn soggy. Place a damp paper towel over the unsalted salsa until you are ready to season and serve it.

TANGY AVOCADO SAUCE {SALSA GUASCA}

Don't be fooled into thinking that this is a pureed guacamole. While most of the ingredients are suspiciously similar, the addition of a small amount of yellow prepared mustard makes all the difference in the world (and no one can ever guess what the secret ingredient is). This tangy sauce has a lusciously creamy texture that complements charred meats perfectly. It also whips up in a flash and goes remarkably well with almost everything. **Makes about 4 cups**

½ red onion, coarsely chopped (about ⅔ cup)
2 cloves garlic, peeled
1 serrano chile, stemmed
½ cup red wine vinegar
¼ cup olive oil
2 teaspoons yellow prepared mustard
½ cup lightly packed cilantro leaves and
    tender stems
4 Hass avocados, pitted and peeled
1 teaspoon salt

PUREE ALL THE INGREDIENTS Place all the ingredients in a blender or food processor and puree until smooth. If using a blender, you may need to push down the ingredients a bit. The finished sauce will have the texture of thick mayonnaise.

COOKING NOTES

INGREDIENTS

Serrano chile For this recipe I like using a serrano chile, which is a bit hotter than a jalapeño chile; the avocados tend to mute the heat. However, use the type and amount of chile that suits your preference, remembering that you can remove any chile's seeds to temper its heat.

ADVANCE PREPARATION

Because the acid in the vinegar and mustard prevents the avocado from turning brown, this recipe can be made a day in advance. To keep it fresh, I place a piece of plastic wrap directly on the surface of the sauce and store it in the refrigerator.

COCONUT RICE {ARROZ CON COCO}

Popular in the beach towns along the Caribbean coast of South America, this easily prepared rice offers a sweet and exotic accompaniment to simply grilled meats. Because the texture of the rice is softened by the coconut milk, I add toasted coconut flakes to provide a crunchy complement. Serves 8

1 tablespoon olive oil
2 cloves garlic, minced
1 onion, chopped (about 1 cup)
1 teaspoon salt
1¾ cups long-grain white rice
1 (13½-ounce) can coconut milk
2 cups water
2 cups sweetened shredded coconut flakes

SAUTÉ THE VEGETABLES AND RICE Place the olive oil and garlic in a medium saucepan over medium-high heat. When the garlic begins to sizzle (after about 40 seconds), add the onion and salt and sauté until the onion becomes limp and translucent, about 4 minutes. Add the rice and stir until all the grains are coated with oil.

SIMMER THE RICE Add the coconut milk and water and bring to a boil. Cover, reduce to a simmer, and cook for 30 minutes, or until all the liquid has been absorbed. Allow the covered pan to sit off the heat for 5 minutes.

TOAST THE COCONUT FLAKES Meanwhile, preheat the oven to 350°F. Place the coconut flakes on a baking sheet and spread out evenly. Bake for 6 minutes, then toss the flakes and evenly spread them out again. Bake for an additional 6 minutes, until the coconut is very fragrant and golden brown. Be careful toward the end of the cooking time, as the coconut can burn very easily. Remove from the oven and remove the coconut flakes from the baking sheet right away to prevent more browning. Set aside.

COOKING NOTES

INGREDIENTS

Coconut milk To get the full coconut flavor, use regular coconut milk and not the light variety. When you open a can of coconut milk, a layer of fat will have accumulated at the top of the can. Just mix it in with the rest of the liquid in the can before using.

ADVANCE PREPARATION

The coconut flakes can be toasted and kept in an airtight container a few days in advance. The rice can be made a few hours in advance and kept at room temperature. In order to maintain the crunchy texture of the coconut flakes, do not toss them with the rice until you are almost ready to serve.

FINISH THE RICE AND SERVE Fluff the rice with a fork and stir in most of the toasted coconut flakes, keeping some to garnish the rice. Transfer the coconut rice to a large serving bowl and sprinkle the remaning coconut flakes on top.

VENEZUELAN CHOCOLATE PUDDING with Espresso Cream

Just as Colombia boasts some of the best coffee plantations in the world, Venezuela produces what is arguably the best chocolate, from the indigenous *criollo* (kree-OH-yoh) cacao plant. Put these two ingredients together and you have the makings of a fabulous dessert. This pudding brings out the best in the rich chocolate and tops it with coffee-infused cream. **Serves 10 to 12**

Chocolate Pudding
4 large egg yolks
1 cup sugar
¼ cup plus 2 tablespoons cornstarch
6 cups whole milk
12 ounces bittersweet (70 percent cacao)
    Venezuelan chocolate or other bittersweet
    chocolate, chopped
¼ teaspoon salt
2 tablespoons vanilla extract

Espresso Cream
2 cups heavy cream, chilled
2 tablespoons sugar
1 tablespoon plus 1 teaspoon instant espresso
    powder

MAKE THE CHOCOLATE MIXTURE Place the egg yolks, sugar, and cornstarch in a medium bowl and beat with a whisk until the ingredients are well combined and the yolks are a light yellow color, about 1 minute.

Place the milk, chocolate, and salt in a medium saucepan and set over medium heat. Stir until the chocolate is completely melted, about 2 minutes. The mixture will look like chocolate milk.

TEMPER THE EGGS Your next step is to combine the chocolate and egg mixtures. However, you need to do so gradually so as not to cook the eggs with the heat of the chocolate. So add about half a cup of the chocolate mixture to the bowl with the egg mixture and stir well. Add another half cup and stir. When the egg mixture feels warm to the touch,

pour it into the pan with the rest of the chocolate and stir to combine.

COOK THE PUDDING Place the chocolate-egg mixture over medium heat and cook, stirring continuously, until the pudding thickens, about 15 minutes. Remove the pan from the heat and stir in the vanilla extract.

COOL THE PUDDING Pour the pudding into a serving dish and allow to cool at room temperature, uncovered, for 20 minutes. Then cover with plastic wrap and refrigerate for 2 hours, or until the pudding has thickened and is chilled through. To prevent a skin forming on the pudding, make sure the plastic wrap touches the pudding's surface.

PREPARE THE COFFEE CREAM In a small bowl, mix the sugar and the instant espresso powder and set aside. Using a handheld electric mixer or stand mixer with the whisk attachment, beat the cream on medium-high speed for 2 minutes, or until it's very frothy. Lower the speed of the mixer and sprinkle in the sugar-espresso mixture. Increase the speed to medium-high and continue beating until the cream has thickened and soft peaks form, about 2 to 3 more minutes.

GARNISH AND SERVE Serve the chilled pudding with dollops of the espresso cream.

INGREDIENTS

Venezuelan chocolate If you cannot find Venezuelan chocolate, look for one made with criollo beans, or simply purchase the best chocolate you can find. The quality of the chocolate makes all the difference in the flavor of the pudding.

Heavy whipping cream Whipping cream has the highest percentage of butterfat in comparison to other creams. This extra fat allows the cream to double in volume and hold its form. In this recipe, you can use either heavy whipping cream or heavy cream with good results. However, half-and-half, sometimes called light cream, will not work.

TECHNIQUE

Whipping cream A cold environment is necessary for cream to whip up with as much volume as possible. If you can, place your mixing bowl and whisk or beaters in the freezer 30 minutes before using them, and make sure your cream is cold.

SERVING SUGGESTION

For a fun presentation, spoon individual portions of the pudding into coffee or espresso cups and top with the cream, as if it were a specialty coffee drink. Then, if you like, garnish with a dusting of cinnamon, cocoa powder, or chocolate shavings.

ADVANCE PREPARATION

The pudding can be made in advance; it will keep for about 4 days in the refrigerator. The cream can be made a few hours in advance and stored in a resealable plastic bag in the refrigerator. When you're ready to serve, snip off the bottom corner of the bag and pipe the cream over the pudding.

The Peruvian Grill

Drink

Pisco Sour {106}

Starters

Ceviche Bar:

Fresh Fish Ceviche with Ginger & Chile / *Ceviche de Pescado* {107}

Shrimp Ceviche / *Ceviche de Camarones* {109}

Mushroom Ceviche / *Ceviche de Hongos* {110}

Crab, Avocado & Potato Terrine / *Causa Limeña* {111}

Main Courses

Soy- & Chile-Marinated Beef Skewers / *Anticuchos* {114}

Chicken Skewers with Spicy Yellow Chile Sauce / *Aji de Gallina* {116}

Sides

Roasted Potatoes with Huancaina Sauce / *Papas a la Huancaina* {119}

Grilled Corn & Quinoa Salad {121}

Dessert

Peruvian Caramel Meringue / *Suspiro de Limeña* {124}

The Inca Indians of Peru are farmers; historically, they have cultivated more than one thousand varieties of potatoes and tubers, as well as grains like quinoa and corn. Spanish colonists, who arrived in the sixteenth century, brought ingredients and techniques—such as beef, eggs, and beans plus herbs and spices such as cilantro and turmeric—that blended with Incan cuisine. Chinese and Japanese inhabitants, who were initially brought to the country in the nineteenth century as indentured workers, have also heavily influenced Peruvian cuisine with ingredients like soy sauce and ginger and techniques like wok cooking and serving raw fish. Some important ingredients of this unique, layered cuisine include corn, potatoes, chiles, sweet potatoes, quinoa, and fish and shellfish.

{MENU GAME PLAN}

One day in advance:
- Prepare the soy and chile marinade. Storage: refrigerator
- Prepare the spicy yellow chile sauce for the chicken. Storage: refrigerator
- Prepare the huancaina sauce for the potatoes. Storage: refrigerator

The night before:
- Prepare the Crab, Avocado & Potato Terrine. Storage: refrigerator
- Prepare the Mushroom Ceviche. Storage: refrigerator
- Prepare the ceviche marinade for the fish. Storage: refrigerator
- Boil the sweet potatoes. Storage: refrigerator
- Prepare the caramel base for dessert. Storage: refrigerator
- Trim and marinate the beef. Storage: refrigerator

On the morning of:
- If you are cooking the corn in the oven, prepare the quinoa salad now. Storage: refrigerator
- Soak the wooden skewers (if using).
- Prepare the shrimp ceviche. Storage: refrigerator

Two to three hours before :
- Add the fish to the ceviche marinade. Storage: refrigerator
- Prepare the potato foil packets. Storage: room temperature
- Thread the chicken and beef onto the skewers. Storage: refrigerator

In the hour before (setup):
- Set up the beverage bar with pisco sour ingredients.
- Set up the ceviche bar serving area—but wait until the last minute to bring out the ceviches.
- Set out:
  Grilled Corn & Quinoa Salad
  Spicy yellow chile sauce
  Huancaina sauce

As your event unfolds:
- Prepare and serve the pisco sours.
- Set out the crab terrine.
- Set out the ceviches.
- Serve the starters.
- If you are grilling the corn for the quinoa salad, do it now.
- Roast and char the potatoes.
- Season the chicken.
- Grill the chicken and beef skewers.
- Serve the main courses.
- Prepare the meringue for dessert.
- Serve dessert.

PISCO SOUR

There is a long-standing dispute between Peru and Chile over which country "owns" the pisco sour. And to complicate matters more, each country produces its own distinct style of pisco, which will impart its particular flavor to the cocktail. Therefore, even when you're using the same recipe, the taste of your pisco sour will vary greatly depending on which country's pisco you used. Whether it's made in the high Andes or Tierra del Fuego, raw egg white is always used to achieve the pisco sour's frothy texture. **Makes 1 cocktail**

Ice
2½ ounces pisco
1 ounce lime juice (from 1 to 2 limes)
½ ounce simple syrup
1 egg white

Fill a cocktail shaker with ice and add all the ingredients. Vigorously shake for 20 to 25 seconds and strain into a chilled martini or short rocks glass.

COOKING NOTES

INGREDIENTS

Pisco Pisco is a distilled spirit made from grapes. It is named after the Peruvian city of Pisco, one of the places where it was first produced.

Simple syrup Simple syrup is a mixture of equal parts water and sugar that has been heated until the sugar melts. It makes a great sweetener for beverages—especially cold ones—since the sugar crystals are already dissolved and will not lend a gritty texture to the drink. I tend to make about 2 cups of it at a time, using 2 cups of sugar and 2 cups of water heated in a saucepan over medium heat. This way, I always have some on hand—it keeps for about 1 month in the refrigerator.

FRESH FISH CEVICHE with Ginger & Chile
{CEVICHE DE PESCADO}

Ceviche is arguably Peru's national dish. It is so popular that throughout the country you will find *cevicherias*—restaurants that specialize in ceviche. In these restaurants you will see all types of fish and shellfish swimming in an assortment of marinades consisting of lime juice, aromatic vegetables, and other ingredients. I've taken inspiration from those ceviche bars and come up with three ceviches that are great to serve as a trio. There's even one that vegetarians or those who do not like raw fish should find irresistible. **Serves 10**

2 pounds mild white fish (such as sea bass, mahi-mahi, halibut, or tilapia), skinned and thinly sliced lengthwise and then cut crosswise (pieces should measure about ¼ thick inch by 1 inch long)
2 cups lime juice (from 24 limes)
1 (4-inch) piece fresh ginger, peeled and grated
1 Peruvian hot pepper (aji amarillo) or habanero chile, stemmed and finely chopped
½ red onion, halved and sliced very thinly
1 cup lightly packed cilantro leaves and tender stems, chopped
Salt
2 sweet potatoes, peeled and cut into 1-inch cubes
1 cup corn nuts

MARINATE THE FISH Place the fish, lime juice, ginger, chile, onion, cilantro, and 1 teaspoon of salt in a bowl and allow to marinate for 30 minutes to 1 hour. There should be enough lime juice that you can completely submerge the fish, which should still have some room to move around a bit in the liquid. This will allow the acid in the lime to fully and evenly penetrate the fish. I like to place a piece of plastic wrap on the surface of the ceviche to assure that the fish remains submerged.

BOIL THE SWEET POTATOES Bring a pot of salted water to a boil. Add the sweet potatoes and cook until fork tender, about 10 minutes. Drain and set aside.

{CONTINUED ON NEXT PAGE}

COOKING NOTES

INGREDIENTS

Peruvian chiles Chiles from Peru are very distinctive. The *aji amarillo* and *rocoto* are two of the most popular. Unfortunately, they are not easily obtained in the United States. Habanero chiles are a good substitute; however, habaneros are hotter, so feel free to use a smaller quantity—or substitute your favorite chile. While you can tame the heat of the chile by removing its veins and seeds, do not eliminate it entirely from the recipe, as it adds a fruity flavor that will be missed if it isn't used.

Sweet potato Boiled sweet potato is often served with ceviche. Its soft texture and sweet flavor complement the bright acid of the ceviche marinade. I also find that it helps to balance the heat from the chiles.

ADVANCE PREPARATION

Peruvian ceviche is not marinated for too long. Possibly as a result of the Japanese influence in Peru, it is often served as soon as the ingredients are mixed, keeping the fish more on the raw side, sashimi style.

You can marinate the fish for as long as you like to achieve the texture and flavor of your preference. However, if you would like to prepare this ahead of time, simply store the uncut fish, prepared lime juice marinade, and boiled sweet potato in separate airtight containers in the refrigerator (you can do this the night before serving). Slice the fish and combine it with the marinade shortly before you are ready to serve.

GARNISH AND SERVE If you're serving the ceviche individually, place a couple of pieces of sweet potato in the bottom of each dish or glass, top with a helping of the ceviche, and drizzle the marinating liquid over the fish. Garnish with a sprinkling of corn nuts.

Alternatively, if you're serving the ceviche on a large platter, place the sweet potato on one side of the platter, drizzle the marinating liquid over the fish, and sprinkle the corn nuts over it.

DON'T FORGET THE LECHE DE TIGRE

The juice that is left on a dish after one eats ceviche is referred to as *leche de tigre,* or tiger's milk. It can be drunk straight from the dish (bringing the dish up to one's mouth is not considered bad manners), or it can be consumed the next day, spiked with a shot of pisco or vodka, as a hangover remedy.

MUSHROOM CEVICHE {CEVICHE DE HONGO}

The mushrooms in this untraditional yet ingenious ceviche are meaty enough to stand up to the acidic marinade without breaking apart, yet they absorb flavors like little sponges. This tangy and flavorful dish can be served as an appetizer or used as a side dish. And this vegetarian-friendly dish is perfect for outdoor entertaining, since you do not have to worry about it getting too warm and becoming unsafe to eat. **Serves 10**

2½ pounds white button mushrooms, stems removed, cut into quarters or eighths (depending on size)
1 cup lime juice (from about 12 limes)
½ cup orange juice (from 1 to 2 oranges)
½ red onion, halved and sliced very thin
1 red bell pepper, cored, seeded, and finely diced
1 cup lightly packed cilantro leaves and tender stems, chopped, plus extra sprigs for garnish
2 teaspoons salt
Black pepper

MARINATE THE MUSHROOMS Combine all the ingredients except the whole cilantro sprigs in a large bowl and allow to marinate for at least 3 hours.

GARNISH AND SERVE Place the ceviche in a large bowl or platter and garnish by topping with the sprigs of fresh cilantro. Serve and enjoy.

COOKING NOTES

INGREDIENTS
Seville orange juice See page 84.

TECHNIQUE
Marinating the mushrooms The mushrooms require at least 3 hours of marinating in order for the acid to "cook out" the raw mushroom flavor and soften their texture.

ADVANCE PREPARATION
This dish needs to be made in advance. You can easily make it up to 24 hours before serving, and it will maintain its freshness for a couple of days after it was prepared.

SHRIMP CEVICHE {CEVICHE DE CAMARONES}

I love this recipe for both its vibrant colors and its fresh flavors. It uses tomato and avocado in addition to the ingredients found in a basic ceviche, giving it texture and color. It is also very versatile: you can substitute any mild white fish for the shrimp. Just keep in mind that shrimp take a bit longer than fish to "cook" in acid, so cut the marinating time in half when substituting fish. **Serves 10**

2 pounds large shrimp, peeled, deveined, and
    butterflied
3 cups lime juice (from about 36 limes)
1 habanero chile or 2 jalapeño chiles, stemmed
    and finely chopped
4 plum tomatoes, cored, seeded, and chopped
½ red onion, halved and sliced very thin
1 cup lightly packed cilantro leaves and tender
    stems, chopped, plus extra sprigs for garnish
2 Hass avocados, peeled, pitted, and chopped
2 teaspoons salt

MARINATE THE SHRIMP AND VEGETABLES Place the shrimp, lime juice, chile, tomatoes, onion, and cilantro in a large bowl and toss well. Cover with plastic wrap and allow to marinate in the refrigerator for at least 2 hours.

GARNISH AND SERVE Shortly before serving, toss in the avocados and season with the salt. Transfer the ceviche to a serving platter and garnish with the sprigs of cilantro. Serve and enjoy.

COOKING NOTES

TECHNIQUES

How to butterfly shrimp A butterflied shrimp is a shrimp that has been sliced lengthwise. Sometimes, one side of the shrimp is kept attached; sometimes it is sliced all the way through. For this recipe, the shrimp will be cut all the way through.

First, peel and devein the shrimp. Then put a shrimp on your cutting board and place the tip of your knife blade in the indentation created on the shrimp's back by the deveining process. Slice the shrimp in half lengthwise, using the indentation as your guide.

Marinating seafood for ceviche There are two things to keep in mind when preparing ceviche: the size of the fish pieces, and the amount of lime juice.

In order for the fish to "cook" evenly, the fish needs to be sliced thin so that the acid from the lime juice can make its way to the center of the flesh. The length of each piece is of less concern; just make sure you keep them bite size.

There should be enough lime juice to completely cover the fish and to allow it to move around a bit in the liquid. If the pieces of fish stick to each other, the acid won't entirely penetrate the pieces. Because the amount of juice found in fresh limes varies considerably, always buy a few more than you think you need.

ADVANCE PREPARATION

This dish needs to be made at least 2 hours in advance. You can prepare it up to 8 hours in advance with little effect on the quality of the dish. However, the tomatoes may become too tart if they stay in the marinade for more than 8 hours.

CRAB, AVOCADO & POTATO TERRINE
{CAUSA LIMEÑA}

I've always considered this Peruvian classic the perfect potato salad. Creamy mashed potatoes, tangy crabmeat salad, and velvety avocado are layered to create a stunningly delicious dish that is deceptively easy to create. Although this combination, which uses crab and avocado, is my favorite, *causas* can be layered with any number of ingredients, such as tuna, ceviche, or tomatoes. **Serves 8**

1½ pounds Yukon gold potatoes
Salt
3 tablespoons butter
½ cup half-and-half
¼ teaspoon cayenne pepper
1 teaspoon turmeric
½ pound lump crabmeat
2 limes
2 green onions, roots trimmed, white and pale green parts thinly sliced
¼ cup lightly packed cilantro leaves and tender stems, finely chopped
2 Hass avocados

PREPARE THE POTATOES Peel the potatoes and place them in a medium pot. Cover the potatoes with cold water, bring to a boil, add ½ teaspoon salt, and cook the potatoes until fork-tender, about 20 minutes.

Drain the potatoes and place in a mixing bowl. Add the butter, half-and-half, cayenne pepper, and turmeric and mash until the potatoes are smooth and creamy. Taste for seasoning and add salt if necessary. Set aside to cool at room temperature.

PREPARE THE CRABMEAT Place the crabmeat in a bowl and pick through it with your fingers to remove any cartilage.

Add the juice of 1 lime, half of the green onion, and the cilantro and toss well. Taste for seasoning and add salt if necessary. Set aside.

COOKING NOTES

INGREDIENTS

Potatoes I like using Yukon gold potatoes for their buttery flavor and creamy texture. For a more dramatic presentation, substitute purple potatoes and eliminate the turmeric.

TECHNIQUE

Boiling potatoes When boiling potatoes, you want to place them in cold water and then bring the pot to a boil. This ensures that the potato cooks evenly: otherwise the inside will still be raw by the time the outer layer is cooked.

ADVANCE PREPARATION

The terrine must be prepared at least 5 hours in advance and can be made up to 1 day in advance.

PREPARE THE AVOCADOS Cut the avocados in half and remove the seeds. Using a spoon, scoop out all of the flesh and place it in a bowl. Add the juice of the other lime and mash. Season with salt and set aside.

ASSEMBLE THE TERRINE Cut a piece of plastic wrap that is long enough to hang over the sides of a 9 by 5-inch loaf pan.

Place half the avocado mixture in the loaf pan and pat it down to an even layer. Create the second layer by spooning the crab mixture over the avocado and spreading it out. Finish the terrine by layering the mashed potato over the crab and smoothing it out.

{CONTINUED}

Fold the plastic wrap over the mashed potato, covering the terrine well. If the potato is not completely covered, place another sheet of plastic over the top of the loaf pan. Refrigerate for at least 5 hours.

GARNISH AND SERVE Have a serving platter ready. Remove the terrine from the refrigerator and open the plastic wrap. Invert the platter over the loaf pan and flip both over so the pan is now upside down on top of the dish. Carefully lift off the loaf pan and peel off the plastic wrap.

Garnish by sprinkling the remaining green onion over the terrine. Gently slice the terrine crosswise, being careful to avoid crumbling the crab layer. I find it best to use a long serrated knife for this and slowly cut through the terrine using a sawing motion.

SOY- & CHILE-MARINATED BEEF SKEWERS
{ANTICUCHOS}

When I think of street food, I immediately think of charred pieces of marinated meat eaten straight off the skewer. I consider *anticuchos* (*ahn-tee-COO-chos*) the quintessential Latin American street food. These highly seasoned grilled beef skewers are found in street carts throughout the Andean region, and while anticuchos can be made from any type of meat, those made from beef hearts are the most popular. For this recipe, however, I decided to go a bit more mainstream and use flank steak instead.
Serves 8

Soy Marinade
¾ cup soy sauce
⅓ cup honey
9 cloves garlic, mashed
2 tablespoons ground cumin
1 tablespoon crushed red pepper flakes

3 pounds flank steak, trimmed of excess fat
2 limes, quartered

SLICE AND MARINATE THE BEEF Place all the marinade ingredients in a large bowl and mix until well combined. Set aside.

Slice the beef against the grain into long strips about ½ inch thick. Place the beef strips in the bowl with the marinade and toss until all the beef is well coated. Cover and allow to marinate, refrigerated, for at least 1 hour.

SKEWER AND GRILL THE BEEF Soak 24 wooden skewers by submerging them completely in water for 20 minutes.

Remove the beef from the marinade and thread 2 pieces onto a soaked skewer. Starting 1 inch from the bottom of a strip of meat and treating the skewer like a needle, make "stitches" in the meat, weaving the skewer in and out every 2 inches or so.

COOKING NOTES

TECHNIQUE

Why soak wooden skewers? Wooden skewers need to be soaked for about 20 minutes to prevent them from catching fire—although they may still smolder and smoke.

ADVANCE PREPARATION

You can prepare the marinade a day in advance and leave the beef marinating for several hours.

Heat your grill to the highest setting and close the lid. Wait at least 15 minutes before continuing.

Oil the grill grates with a vegetable oil–soaked paper towel held with a long pair of tongs. Grill the skewers for 3 to 4 minutes per side. Lower the lid if desired, but just keep in mind that because the beef is sliced thin it will cook quickly.

SERVE Transfer the beef skewers to a serving platter and garnish with the lime wedges.

CHICKEN SKEWERS
with Spicy Yellow Chile Sauce {AJI DE GALLINA}

Aji de gallina (ah-HEE-deh-gah-YEE-nah) is one of Peru's most emblematic dishes. Traditionally, the dish is made by stewing then shredding a whole chicken and tossing the meat in the yellow chile sauce. The chile sauce is made with the Peruvian chile aji amarillo and other aromatics, which are blended with a bit of evaporated milk. This spicy-hot and flavorful sauce is so delicious, versatile, and easy to prepare that I've often wondered why it's not paired with other meats. So I reworked this classic by grilling skewered chicken breast meat and serving the sauce on the side, which gives you the option of using it with other grilled meats and seafood. **Serves 8**

Spicy Yellow Chile Sauce
2 tablespoons vegetable oil
3 cloves garlic, peeled and crushed
1 onion, chopped
1 serrano or habanero chile, stemmed and
    chopped
2 teaspoons turmeric
Salt
½ cup evaporated milk
¼ cup walnut pieces
1 lime

2 pounds skinless, boneless chicken breasts
¼ cup vegetable oil
Salt and black pepper
3 limes, cut into wedges

SOAK THE SKEWERS Soak 24 wooden skewers by submerging them completely in water for 20 minutes.

PREPARE THE SAUCE Put the oil and garlic in a medium sauté pan and set over medium-high heat. When the garlic begins to sizzle (after about 40 seconds), add the onion, chile, turmeric, and ½ teaspoon of salt and sauté until the vegetables become limp and translucent, about 5 minutes.

Transfer the sautéed vegetables to a blender and add the evaporated milk and walnuts. Puree until smooth. Add the juice of 1 lime and taste for seasoning. Set aside.

SLICE, SEASON, AND SKEWER THE CHICKEN Slice the chicken against the grain into long strips, each about 1 inch thick. Drizzle with vegetable oil and season with salt and pepper.

Remove the skewers from the water and thread the chicken strips onto the skewers. Starting 1 inch from the bottom of each strip and treating the skewer like a needle, make "stitches" in the meat, weaving the skewer in and out every 2 inches or so.

GRILL THE CHICKEN Heat your grill to high (550°F) and close the lid. Wait at least 15 minutes before lowering the heat to medium-high (450°F) and continuing.

Oil the grill grates with a vegetable oil–soaked paper towel held with a long pair of tongs. Place the skewers on the grill, lower the lid, and cook for 7 minutes, or until the bottom of the chicken develops grill marks and turns golden brown. Turn the skewers over. Leaving the lid open, grill for another 7 minutes or until the chicken is cooked through.

SERVE Place the grilled chicken skewers on a serving platter and garnish with lime wedges. You can drizzle yellow chile sauce over the skewers or allow your guests to do so themselves.

COOKING NOTES

INGREDIENTS

Chiles The Peruvian yellow chile (aji amarillo) is traditionally used in this recipe. However, since they are not always readily available, I am substituting a serrano chile or habanero chile in its place. Although it's still plenty hot, the serrano is a bit milder than the habanero; both are hotter than the aji amarillo.

ADVANCE PREPARATION

The sauce can be prepared a day in advance and will keep refrigerated in an airtight container for about a week.

The chicken can be skewered several hours in advance, but wait until right before grilling to season it with salt and pepper.

ROASTED POTATOES with Huancaina Sauce
{PAPAS A LA HUANCAINA}

Although the sauce is named after Huancayo, the capital of Peru's central highlands, this potato dish has come to represent classic Peruvian home cooking and is enjoyed all over the country. Traditionally, the sauce is used to smother boiled potatoes. I have added my own twist to this classic, roasting the potatoes in foil packets on the grill to give them some texture. This tangy, creamy, spicy sauce can be used to accompany many other dishes, but it pairs especially well with seafood. **Serves 8**

Sauce
2 tablespoons vegetable oil
2 cloves garlic, chopped
1 small onion, chopped
1 serrano chile, stemmed and chopped
2 teaspoons turmeric
Salt
¼ cup plus 2 tablespoons evaporated milk
4 ounces goat cheese
1 hard-boiled egg, peeled and chopped

3 pounds small red potatoes, cut into quarters
½ cup olive oil
Salt and black pepper

--- COOKING NOTES ---

INGREDIENTS

Chiles The Peruvian yellow chile aji amarillo is traditionally used to make this sauce spicy hot. However, since these are not always readily available, I am substituting a serrano chile in its place.

ADVANCE PREPARATION

The sauce can be made a day in advance and it keeps, refrigerated, for a few days. The potato packets can be assembled a few hours in advance and kept at room temperature.

PREPARE THE SAUCE Place the oil and garlic in a medium sauté pan and set over medium-high heat. When the garlic begins to sizzle (after about 40 seconds), add the onion, chile, turmeric, and ½ teaspoon of salt and sauté until the vegetables become limp and translucent, about 5 minutes.

Transfer the sautéed vegetables to a blender and add the evaporated milk, goat cheese, and egg. Puree until smooth. Taste for seasoning and add more salt if necessary. The sauce should have the consistency of creamy salad dressing. If you need to thin it out, add a bit more evaporated milk. Set aside.

PREPARE FOIL PACKETS OF POTATOES Cut a piece of foil about 14 inches in length and place ¼ of the potatoes in its center. Drizzle 2 tablespoons of olive oil onto the potatoes and toss gently to coat well. Season with salt and pepper.

Create a square packet by bringing the long sides of the foil up toward the center and folding the edges over a couple of times to create a seal. Bring the ends up towards the center and seal by crimping the foil shut. Repeat the process three times to end up with a total of four packets.

{CONTINUED}

ROAST THE POTATOES Heat your grill to high (550°F) and close the lid. Wait at least 15 minutes before lowering the heat to medium-high (450°F) and continuing.

Place the potato packets on the grill shelf and close the lid. Allow the potatoes to roast for 40 minutes, or until tender. I test this by skewering the tip of a thin knife through the foil and into a potato. If I don't meet resistance, the potatoes are ready. If you do not have a grill shelf, lower the heat to medium and place the packets directly on the grates.

CHAR THE POTATOES Increase the grill heat to high (550°F). Place the packets directly on the grates, close the lid, and allow to cook for 15 minutes to char the bottom of the potatoes. Remove the packets from the grill and set aside to cool.

SERVE Open the packets, being careful not to burn yourself with the steam, and transfer the potatoes to a serving bowl. You may need to peel off some of the potatoes that have become stuck and charred to the foil. (If the potatoes have not developed a charred crust, close the foil packet and return to the grill until a crust develops.) Traditionally, this dish is served with the sauce already drizzled over the potatoes. However, you may want to serve the sauce on the side, allowing your guests to serve themselves.

GRILLED CORN AND QUINOA SALAD

Quinoa has been a staple grain in Peru for centuries. Highly nutritious, it is a complete protein that is high in iron and fiber, and it has a very mild flavor that complements anything it is paired with. And, when you consider that it cooks in only 15 minutes, you understand why it's called the "gold of the Incas." **Serves 8 to 10**

5 ears corn, husks on but silks removed (see page 33)
4 green onions, roots and tops trimmed
2 cups quinoa, well rinsed
3¼ cups water
Salt
4 plum tomatoes, cored, seeded, and diced
1 cup lightly packed cilantro leaves and tender stems, chopped
Juice of 3 limes (about ¼ cup)
2 tablespoons olive oil
Black pepper

SOAK THE CORN Place the corn in a large stockpot, or other container large enough to hold all the ears, and fill it with water. If you do not have a sufficiently large container, use your kitchen sink.

Allow the corn to soak for 20 minutes. Remove from the water, shake, and tightly squeeze the husks against the kernels of corn to get rid of any excess water.

GRILL THE CORN Heat your grill to high (550°F) and close the lid. Wait at least 15 minutes before lowering the heat to medium-high (450°F) and continuing. (Or see Cooking Notes, right, for instructions on roasting the corn in an oven.)

Place the corn on the grill rack, close the lid, and grill for 5 minutes. Turn the corn over and grill for another 5 minutes with the lid closed. Remove from the grill and let rest for 5 more minutes.

{CONTINUED ON NEXT PAGE}

COOKING NOTES

TECHNIQUES

Cooking quinoa Quinoa should always be rinsed well under cold running water before it's cooked; otherwise it will have a rather bitter taste.

Package instructions for preparing quinoa state that you should use 2 cups of liquid to 1 cup of quinoa. I find this ratio results in a soggy texture that does not work well in a grain salad. Therefore, this recipe uses a proportion of approximately 1½ cups of liquid to 1 cup of grain in order to end up with a grain that will stay intact when tossed with the vinaigrette and vegetables.

Roasting the corn in the oven This recipe can easily be made in the oven using corn kernels that have been removed from the cob, or 3 cups of frozen corn that has been thawed. Preheat your oven to 400°F. Roast the corn in a single layer on a baking sheet for 20 minutes, then allow to rest outside the oven for another 5 minutes. If you like, the green onions can just be left raw or can be roasted with the corn.

ADVANCE PREPARATION

This recipe can be made a day in advance and kept in an airtight container in the refrigerator. Bring to room temperature before serving.

PULL BACK THE HUSKS AND CHAR THE CORN Take the grilled ears of corn and pull back the husks, exposing the kernels. Do not remove the husks. If possible, tie the husks back (see Cooking Notes page 33).

Increase the grill temperature to high (550°F). Place a sheet of aluminum foil on one side of the hot grill. Place the pulled-back husks over the foil, allowing the exposed kernels to sit on the grill grates. (This is done so the husks don't burn before the corn can char.)

Close the grill lid and allow the kernels to char for about 5 minutes per side, or until they become dark and golden brown on all sides. At this point, add the green onions to the grill and char on all sides, about 8 minutes total. Remove the corn and green onions from the grill and set aside.

PREPARE THE QUINOA Put the quinoa, water, and 1 teaspoon salt in a saucepan. Bring to a boil, cover, and lower to a simmer. Cook for 15 minutes.

Uncover and check if the quinoa is ready by tilting the pan to the side to make sure all the water has been absorbed. If not, continue cooking for a few minutes more.

Transfer the cooked quinoa to a large bowl and allow to cool at room temperature.

TOSS AND DRESS THE SALAD AND SERVE Cut the corn kernels off the cobs, slice the grilled green onions, and add both to the quinoa. Toss in the tomatoes and cilantro and mix well. Drizzle the lime juice and olive oil over the salad and season with salt and pepper to taste. Toss well before serving.

PERUVIAN CARAMEL MERINGUE
{SUSPIRO DE LIMEÑA}

Composed of light dollops of meringue left to float atop a sweet liquid base, *suspiro de limeña* is a cousin of the floating island dessert. The dish, whose name literally translates to "the lady from Lima sighs," is one of Peru's most popular desserts and will make any man or woman sigh with satisfaction upon tasting it. **Serves 8 to 10**

3 eggs, separated
2 teaspoons vanilla extract
½ cup (7½ ounces, or half a can) sweetened
    condensed milk
1 (12-ounce) can evaporated milk
Pinch of salt
2 tablespoons confectioners' sugar
2 tablespoons port wine
Ground cinnamon, for dusting

PREPARE THE BASE Beat the egg yolks in a small bowl with a fork until light yellow in color. Mix in the vanilla. Set aside.

Place the condensed milk and evaporated milk in a saucepan and stir well to fully combine. Set the pan over high heat and bring to a boil. Immediately lower to a simmer and cook for 20 minutes, occasionally stirring with a rubber spatula and making sure to scrape the bottom of the pan. You will notice the milk thickening along the walls of the pan. Scrape it off and stir it into the milk mixture; it will contribute to the thickening of the base.

The mixture is ready when the bottom of the pan can easily be seen when stirring the milk—it should not immediately flow back into the furrow made by the spatula. At this point the mixture will have darkened to a deep caramel color.

TEMPER THE EGGS Remove the pan from the heat. Add a small amount (about ¼ cup) of the hot milk mixture to the beaten egg yolks and stir until combined. Then add another ¼ cup of the milk to the yolks. You are mixing the egg and milk slowly to keep the eggs from cooking when they come in contact with the hot milk. When the egg mixture feels warm to the touch, add it to the pan holding the remaining milk and stir to combine well.

THICKEN THE BASE Set the pan over medium heat and cook for 2 minutes, while stirring, to allow the mixture to thicken a bit more. At this point the custard should have the consistency of a thin pudding. Remove from the heat and set aside. The custard will thicken more as it cools. Ultimately, it should have the viscosity of a caramel sauce.

PREPARE THE MERINGUE Using a stand mixer with the whisk attachment or a handheld electric mixer, beat the egg whites at medium-high speed until frothy, about 2 minutes. Add the confectioners' sugar and continue beating on high until the egg whites form stiff peaks, 4 to 6 minutes, depending on your mixer.

SERVE THE DESSERT To serve the dessert family style, pour the thickened base into a shallow serving bowl. Top with dollops of meringue and lightly drizzle the port wine over all. Garnish with a dusting of ground cinnamon

This dessert looks stunning when served in individual portions. The trick is to use a glass vessel, such as a wine goblet or martini glass. For this presentation, pour two large spoonfuls of the custard base into the glass and top with a large "sigh," or dollop, of meringue. Finish with a drizzle of port wine and a dusting of ground cinnamon.

COOKING NOTES

TECHNIQUE

Tempering eggs This technique is used in order to add eggs to hot or warm mixtures without the eggs cooking in the process. Just add small amounts of the hot liquid to the eggs to slowly increase the temperature of the eggs. As soon as the eggs feel warm to the touch, they are safe to add to a warm liquid.

ADVANCE PREPARATION

The base can be made a day in advance and kept refrigerated in an airtight container. The meringue should be made shortly before serving in order to maintain its full volume and light texture.

Patagonian Asado

Drinks

Beer

Rustic Red Wine

Starters

Olives, Cheese & Spanish Chorizo /
Picadita de Queso y Chorizo {128}

Grilled Chorizo with Crusty
Bread / *Choripan* {130}

Main Course

Bounty of Wood-Smoked Meats: Boneless
Short Ribs, Skirt Steak, Chicken /
Parrillada: Tira de Asado, Entraña, Pollo {131}

Sides

Arugula Salad with Crunchy
Charred Potatoes {135}

Grilled Endive, Green Onions
& Tomatoes {137}

Dessert

Dulce de Leche Flan {138}

Patagonia is the southernmost portion of South America—it's located mostly in Argentina, but also extends into Chile. The cuisine of the region is very similar to that of Argentina; it is highly focused on grilled meats and game and locally sourced vegetables like green onions, potatoes, and carrots that grow well in its cold climate. Its rugged outdoor culture inspires outdoor cooking methods, especially charcoal grilling and wood smoking, although open spit roasting is still the time-honored favorite. Wine making is a bourgeoning industry in this area of South America, which many refer to as the end of the world. Merlot and chardonnay have been found to grow well in this region, but many locals still favor Argentina's signature grape, malbec.

{MENU GAME PLAN}

The night before:
- Prepare the Dulce de Leche Flan. Storage: refrigerator

On the morning of:
- Soak the wood chips.

Two to three hours before:
- Prepare the tray of Olives, Cheese & Spanish Chorizo. Storage: room temperature
- Prepare foil packets of potatoes for the salad. Storage: room temperature
- Trim and portion the meats. Storage: refrigerator

- Prepare the salad dressing. Storage: room temperature
- Wash and trim the endives, green onions, and tomatoes. Cover with a damp towel. Storage: room temperature

In the hour before (setup):
- Set up the beverage bar with beer and wine.
- Set out the chorizo and prepare the bread for Grilled Chorizo with Crusty Bread.
- Prepare 3 foil packets of wood chips.
- Set out: Olives, Cheese & Spanish Chorizo

As your event unfolds:
- Grill the chorizo and bread.
- Serve the starters.
- Roast the potatoes.
- Grill the endive, green onions, and tomatoes.
- Char the potatoes.
- Place the foil packets of wood chips in the grill to begin smoking.
- Grill/smoke the meats.
- Toss the salad with the charred potatoes and dressing.
- Serve the main courses and sides.
- Serve dessert.

OLIVES, CHEESE & SPANISH CHORIZO
{PICADITA DE QUESO Y CHORIZO}

The easiest things are often overlooked. Few starters are more inviting than a tray of cheese, chorizo, and olives, and even fewer are easier to prepare. An offering of *picadita* (little pickings) and a glass of robust red wine is the way many meals begin in the Southern Cone, the triangular region in the southernmost tip of South America made up of Chile, Argentina, and Uruguay. **Serves 8**

1 (½-pound) wedge Parmesan cheese
½ pound provolone cheese, sliced
1 pound Spanish chorizo, sliced very thin
1 cup mixed olives

ASSEMBLE THE TRAY AND SERVE Place the cheeses and the chorizo on a cheese board or serving tray. Include a hard cheese knife, with a wedge-shaped blade, to chip off chunks of the Parmesan.

Place the olives in a separate small bowl and set a smaller dish next to it to collect the pits.

--- COOKING NOTES ---

INGREDIENTS

Spanish chorizo Because most Spanish chorizos are smoked and cured, they can be eaten straight from the package, making them great snacking sausages (fresh chorizo needs to be cooked first). This pork sausage is flavored with Spanish paprika and garlic, giving it its characteristic reddish color and highly spiced flavor.

Provolone Provolone is an Italian cow's milk cheese that comes in sharp and mild varieties. I prefer the piquancy of sharp provolone.

ADVANCE PREPARATION

Because the cheese and chorizo are best eaten at room temperature, I recommend you assemble the tray a few hours before serving and cover the tray with plastic wrap while you are waiting to serve.

GRILLED CHORIZO SKEWERS
with Crusty Bread {CHORIPAN}

Choripan, short for chorizo-*pan* (*pan* is Spanish for *bread*), is simply grilled fresh chorizo sausage served with a piece of bread. As soon as the chorizo is off the grill, I slice it on top of the crusty bread to collect any juice that may spill out during the slicing, then I stab a skewer in it and hand it over to a guest. I love Spanish chorizo with its smoked paprika flavor, but use your favorite fresh sausage in this dish. Paired with a glass of red wine, it's the perfect starter for a leisurely Patagonian cookout. **Serves 8**

1 baguette
Olive oil
Salt and black pepper
1½ pounds fresh chorizo

PREPARE THE BREAD Slice the bread lengthwise into 2 pieces. Drizzle olive oil over the cut side of each half and season with salt and pepper. Set aside.

GRILL THE CHORIZO Heat your grill to high (550°F) and close the lid. Wait at least 15 minutes before lowering the heat to medium-high (450°F) and continuing. Oil the grill grates with a vegetable oil–soaked paper towel held with a long pair of tongs.

Place the chorizo directly on the grill and cook for 15 minutes per side. The sausage should look somewhat charred. Remove from the grill and set aside.

GRILL THE BREAD Place the bread cut side down on the grill and cook for 5 minutes, or until the bread develops grill marks and turns golden brown.

SERVE Place the chorizo on one half of the grilled bread and insert wooden skewers 3 inches apart from each other. Slice the chorizo in between the skewers, creating 3-inch-long skewered pieces of chorizo and bread. Place on a platter and allow your guests to help themselves.

COOKING NOTES

INGREDIENTS

Chorizo Chorizo is a pork sausage characterized by its red color. This highly seasoned sausage owes its color to either smoked paprika or chile peppers. Fresh chorizo is available at many markets, but you can substitute spicy Italian sausage if you like.

ADVANCE PREPARATION

You can prepare the bread with the oil and seasonings 1 hour in advance. However, it is best to grill the chorizo and bread right before serving to maintain the dish's juicy and crispy nature.

BOUNTY OF WOOD-SMOKED MEATS:
Boneless Short Ribs, Skirt Steak, Chicken
{PARRILLADA: TIRA DE ASADO, ENTRAÑA, POLLO}

For many, including myself, grilling over a wood fire is as good as it gets. I don't know if it's the primitive satisfaction of cooking over flames, the seductive aroma of the charring wood, or the deep, smoky flavor that is infused into the meats, but the appeal is undeniable. In the Patagonian countryside, wood fire grilling is part of a way of life. For those of us outside that region, unfortunately, it can be logistically tricky. Luckily, using wood chips over a gas or charcoal fire can give us a semblance of the real thing. I know it's not the same as cooking over smoky logs at an Argentine ranch, but until you can make it down there, this is an easy and convenient option. **Serves 8**

2 pounds boneless, skinless chicken breasts
2 pounds skirt steak, trimmed of excess fat
2 pounds boneless beef short ribs
Salt and black pepper

SOAK THE WOOD CHIPS Place 3 handfuls of wood chips in a bowl filled with water and push them under the water a few times to help start the soaking process. Allow the chips to soak for 1 hour, then drain.

PREPARE FOIL PACKETS OF CHIPS AND START SMOKING THE WOOD Cut three 16-inch squares of foil and place a handful of the soaked wood chips in the center of each, making sure to spread the chips out a bit. Fold the sides of the foil over the top, creating packets that are sealed tightly. Using the tip of a sharp knife, make small slits all over the top of the foil packet.

Place the foil packets under the grill grates. If possible, place the packets so they will not be sitting directly under the meat (for example, at the back of the grill). Turn the grill on to the highest setting, close the lid, and wait for the wood to begin to smoke. It should take about 10 to 15 minutes but will vary with your grill. You should see smoke escaping from the sides of the grill when it's ready.

{CONTINUED ON NEXT PAGE}

COOKING NOTES

EQUIPMENT

Wood chips Convenient and easy to use, these small pieces of wood are great for adding a smoky flavor to grilled meats, fish, and vegetables.

In order to prevent the chips from burning and turning your food bitter, soak them before using. If your grill has a smoker or if you are using a grill-top smoker, read the directions before using; otherwise follow the directions in the recipe for creating foil packets of chips for smoking.

I tend to use hickory, apple, or cherrywood chips. The hickory gives the meat a more intense smoky flavor, while the cherry and apple are a bit milder.

Aluminum foil It's best to use heavy-duty aluminum foil for the packets; however, you can substitute two layers of regular foil.

SEASON AND GRILL THE MEATS Oil the grill grates with a vegetable oil–soaked paper towel held with a long pair of tongs.

Season the meats with salt and pepper and place the meats on the grill. Close the lid and lower the heat to medium-high. Cook the meats for 6 minutes undisturbed, with the lid closed in order to maintain the smoke in the grill. At this point, the meats should have developed grill marks and a brown or tan hue from the smoke. Turn the meats over, close the lid, and cook for another 6 minutes. Take the internal temperature of the meats and remove from the grill when the chicken registers 160°F and the beef 130°F for medium-rare, or continue cooking until you reach your desired level of doneness (refer to chart on page 10).

SERVE Serve all the cuts of meat on a large tray, preferably a wooden one equipped with a sharp knife and carving fork, so guests can slice off their own pieces of meat.

COOKING NOTES

TECHNIQUE

Flare-ups Flare-ups tend to occur when you are grilling fatty cuts of meat (like the short ribs in this recipe) over high heat, or when oil from a marinade drips into the flames.

Do not try to extinguish a flare-up with water—it won't work. It's best to move your meat away from the flames and let the fire burn out on its own—even if you have to stack some of the meat on top of other pieces that are situated away from the flare-up.

ADVANCE PREPARATION

The foil packets can be made a few hours in advance.

BAKE THE FLAN Pour the flan mixture over the caramel in the bottom of the pan. Carefully place the pan in the center of the water bath. You may hear the hardened caramel crack—that's okay.

Bake for 1½ hours, or until a cake tester, toothpick, or butter knife inserted in the center of the flan comes out clean. The center will still jiggle a bit.

Remove the loaf pan from the oven and allow it to cool at room temperature for 30 minutes before placing it in the refrigerator to chill for at least an hour, or overnight. By now the water-filled roasting pan in the oven will have cooled a bit; remove it from the oven and discard the water.

UNMOLD THE FLAN Before you unmold the flan, the bottom of the loaf pan needs to be heated to melt the caramel a bit. Turn a burner of your range on to medium-high and let the pan sit on the range top until you hear the caramel crack. Move the pan over the heat a few times to make sure both ends of the pan have been heated. This should take a couple of minutes.

Run a thin knife blade around the sides of the pan. Invert a serving platter over the loaf pan and flip both over, dislodging the flan from the pan. Some of the caramel will drip down the sides of the flan onto the platter. A good amount of caramel will have remained in its solid state in the pan, which is to be expected. Simply discard it.

SERVE Slice the flan into 1-inch-thick pieces, place on individual plates, and enjoy.

MAKING DULCE DE LECHE

It is not difficult to make your own dulce de leche; it just requires time and a little attention. Place an unopened can of sweetened condensed milk at the bottom of a very large pot filled with water. (You will need to use two 14-ounce cans to get enough dulce de leche to use in this flan recipe; you'll have a little bit left over.) The can should be completely submerged. Bring the water to a boil, turn the heat down, and allow it to simmer uncovered for 2½ hours. Make sure the can is always covered with water and add hot water to the pot as soon as you see the water level skimming the top of the can. Keeping the can submerged in water ensures that the milk will cook and caramelize evenly. While there is no danger if the water level drops below the top of the can, the can may burst if the pan goes dry.

Once the milk has finished cooking, move the pot into the sink and run cold water into it to cool the can. Take the can out of the pot and let it cool at room temperature for 30 minutes. Open the can only after it has cooled completely in order to keep the hot dulce de leche from bursting out.

Argentine Grill

Drink

Rustic Red Wine

Starters

Grilled Provolone Cheese / *Provoleta* {142}

Beef Empanadas and Sausage &
Mushroom Empanadas {143}

Grilled Rosemary Flatbread {147}

Main Course

Arugula-, Garlic- & Green Onion–
Stuffed Flank Steak / *Matambre*
Beef Empanadas and Sausage &
Mushroom Empanadas {149}

Condiments & Sides

Fresh Parsley Sauce / *Chimichurri* {152}

Char-Grilled Vegetables {153}

Savory Corn Pudding / *Humita de Olla* {154}

Dessert

Dulce de Leche Cookie Cake /
Alfajor Gigante {156}

When it comes to Argentine cuisine, most people immediately think of beef. And with good reason: Argentina is a large country with extensive grazing land, and Argentine beef is wildly popular at home and famous abroad for its delicious grass-fed flavor. But Argentine cuisine is also highly influenced by European immigrants, most notably those from Italy, France, Germany, and Britain. In fact, it is as a whole less fiery and more reminiscent of European cuisines than other Latin American cuisines. And beef isn't the only meat Argentines enjoy; lamb and pig are also popular, as are a wide range of sausages. Other important elements of Argentine cooking include aromatics like parsley, fresh oregano, and garlic; sweet corn; and the thick sweet caramelized-milk sauce known as dulce de leche. Argentina is an important wine-producing and wine-exporting country, with malbec as the grape the industry was founded on in this region. However, Argentina is also a large producer and consumer of cabernet sauvignon and chardonnay.

{MENU GAME PLAN}

One day in advance:
- Make the Dulce de Leche Cookie Cake, but do not dust with confectioners' sugar yet. Cover in plastic wrap. Storage: room temperature

The night before:
- Prepare and assemble the empanadas, but do not bake yet. Wrap well in plastic wrap. Storage: refrigerator
- Prepare the flatbread dough. Cover in plastic wrap. Storage: refrigerator

On the morning of:
- Coat the provolone in breadcrumbs and cover tightly in plastic wrap. Storage: freezer
- Prepare the Chimichurri. Storage: refrigerator
- Cut and prepare the vegetables for char-grilling. Cover with a damp towel. Storage: room temperature

Two to three hours before:
- Prepare the Savory Corn Pudding and leave in a covered pot. Storage: room temperature
- Assemble, roll, and tie the flank steak. Wrap tightly in plastic wrap or foil. Storage: refrigerator

In the hour before (setup):
- Set up the beverage bar.
- Bring the empanadas to room temperature and brush with egg.
- Bring the flatbread dough to room temperature. Prepare the rosemary basting brush.
- Dust the Dulce de Leche Cookie Cake with confectioners' sugar.
- Bring out the frozen provolone cheese 20 minutes before you're ready to grill it.
- Set out: Chimichurri

As your event unfolds:
- Grill the empanadas (or, if you are short on grill space, you can bake them in the oven).
- Roll out and grill the rosemary flatbread.
- Grill the provolone cheese.
- Serve the starters.
- Char-grill the vegetables.
- Reheat the Savory Corn Pudding.
- Grill the flank steak.
- Serve the main courses and sides.
- Serve dessert.

GRILLED PROVOLONE CHEESE {PROVOLETA}

When I first visited Argentina, the one dish that stood out among the rest was the *provoleta* I had at the famed Cabaña las Lilas in Buenos Aires. A thick slab of provolone cheese was grilled until its exterior was burnt and crisp and its interior was soft and gooey. How they were able to grill the cheese without creating a catastrophic mess all over the grill, much less produce a crispy texture on the outside of the cheese, was mind-blowing to me. I immediately asked everyone I could how it was done. Waiters, cooks, friends, acquaintances all told me the secret was the cheese, which could only be found in Argentina. Defeated, I accepted that I would have to make special trips for this delicious dish. Futile attempts at making it at home resulted in disaster.

Then one day I had an "ah-ha!" moment. I was getting ready to grate some mozzarella to fill some empanadas, and I briefly placed the cheese in the freezer to make it easier to shred. That's when it occurred to me: *freeze* the provolone before grilling it. It worked! This recipe, which I coat with breadcrumbs laced with oregano, has the same texture as the one I had at Cabaña las Lilas. **Serves 8**

All-purpose flour
1 egg
½ cup panko (Japanese breadcrumbs)
1 tablespoon dried oregano
½ pound provolone, in 1 (1-inch-thick) piece,
    at room temperature
Bread sticks, store bought
Crackers, store bought
Rosemary flatbread (page 147)

COAT THE PROVOLONE AND FREEZE Place three shallow dishes side by side. Put ⅓ cup flour in one, crack and lightly beat the egg in another, and combine the panko and oregano in the third.

Dredge the provolone in the flour so that all the surfaces are floured. Then dip it into the egg, and finally coat it well with the oregano-panko mixture, patting the crumbs onto the cheese. Wrap the coated provolone with plastic wrap and put in the freezer for 1 hour.

GRILL AND SERVE THE PROVOLONE Heat your grill to high (550°F) and close the lid. Wait at least 15 minutes before continuing. Oil the grill grates with a vegetable oil–soaked paper towel held with a long pair of tongs.

COOKING NOTES

INGREDIENTS

Panko Also called Japanese breadcrumbs, panko is lighter and flakier than typical Italian-style breadcrumbs. I use them here to give the crust of the cheese a light, crispy texture.

ADVANCE PREPARATION

The cheese can be coated in the breadcrumb mixture, covered in plastic, and frozen several hours before grilling.

Remove the cheese from the plastic wrap and place it on the grill, leaving the lid open. Cook until the bottom of the cheese develops grill marks and turns golden brown, about 4 minutes, and then flip. Grill for another 4 minutes. Transfer to a cheese board and serve immediately with bread sticks, crackers, and rosemary flatbread.

BEEF EMPANADAS and SAUSAGE & MUSHROOM EMPANADAS

Many consider the empanada to be the national dish of Argentina—it seems they are eaten all over the country at all hours of the day. These small handheld pies can be filled with any number of ingredients, but the most popular filling is beef. The beef empanada is definitely a crowd pleaser, but I also love them filled with sausage and mushrooms. Both make perfect snacks to serve your guests while they enjoy a glass of wine before a meal. Empanadas are usually baked, sometimes fried, but never grilled—until now. I tried grilling them as an experiment, and I am so glad I did, as grilled empanadas have now become a staple at all my football- (or *futból*) watching parties. **Makes 16 empanadas**

Empanada Dough
3 cups all-purpose flour
½ cup vegetable shortening
⅔ cup water
1½ teaspoons salt
1 egg, lightly beaten

Beef Filling
Olive oil
1 pound boneless sirloin, finely diced
Salt
2 tablespoons butter
1 onion, chopped fine
1 teaspoon smoked paprika
½ teaspoon ground cumin

Sausage Filling
1 tablespoon olive oil
2 fresh sausage links (about ½ pound total), casings removed and crumbled
½ onion, chopped fine
½ pound cremini mushrooms, chopped fine
Salt

1 egg, for egg wash

PREPARE THE DOUGH Place the flour in a large bowl. Combine the vegetable shortening, water, and salt in a small saucepan and cook over medium heat until the shortening has melted, 1 to 2 minutes, stirring to combine.

Pour the melted shortening mixture over the flour, add the egg, and stir to combine. The flour mixture will be clumpy, and you may not be able to stir much with a spoon. Using your hands, begin to work the dough in the bowl until you are able to create a ball. The dough will be pretty dry and a bit crumbly. Transfer the dough to a lightly floured work surface and knead with your hands for about 4 minutes, or until you feel the dough become smooth and elastic. The dough will not be sticky.

Wrap the dough in plastic wrap and allow it to rest at room temperature for 30 minutes. If you are not going to be using the dough for more than

{CONTINUED}

"In order to distinguish the empanadas after they have been closed, I like to create a different seal for each filling."

an hour, refrigerate it. (But bring it back to room temperature before you start rolling and cutting it.)

PREPARE THE BEEF FILLING Place a medium skillet over medium-high heat and add 1 tablespoon of olive oil. Put about ¼ of the diced beef in the pan, spreading it across the bottom of the pan. If you add too much meat to the pan or crowd it, the beef will steam and not brown. Season with a pinch of salt and turn the meat with a spatula to brown on all sides. As soon as the meat is browned, about 5 minutes, remove it from the pan with a slotted spatula or spoon and place it on a dish. Repeat with batches of the remaining beef until it's all browned, adding more olive oil as needed.

Lower the heat under the pan to medium and add the butter. When the butter has melted, add the onion, paprika, and cumin and stir to coat the onion with butter and spices. Sauté the onion until it becomes limp and translucent, about 4 minutes.

Take the pan off the heat, add the beef, and stir to combine well with the onion mixture. Transfer the beef mixture to a dish and set aside. Wipe the skillet down to use for the sausage filling.

PREPARE THE SAUSAGE FILLING Place the skillet over medium-high heat and add the olive oil. When the oil is hot, add the sausage and the onion and cook, breaking apart the sausage meat, until the meat begins to render its fat, about 4 minutes. Add the mushrooms, season with a pinch of salt, and continue cooking until the mixture is well blended and cooked through, about another 6 minutes. Taste for seasoning and adjust if needed.

ROLL OUT AND CUT THE DOUGH Cut the empanada dough in half. Keep one half wrapped in plastic and place the other on a floured work surface in front of you. Using a rolling pin, roll out the dough to about ⅛ inch thick. To keep the dough from sticking, lift it up off the work surface after every couple of rolls.

Use a 4-inch-diameter round cookie cutter or the rim of a glass to cut out circles of dough. You should get about 8 circles (you may need to reroll the dough once to make enough). Make sure to cover the dough circles with plastic wrap while you work to keep them from drying out. If you want to stack them, place a piece of parchment paper between the layers to keep the dough circles from sticking to each other. Repeat with the other half of the dough.

ASSEMBLE AND SEAL THE EMPANADAS Place a circle of dough in front of you and place a couple of tablespoons of filling in the center of the circle. Wet your fingers with water and use them to lightly wet the edges of the dough circle. Fold one side of the dough over, closing the empanada and concealing the filling.

In order to distinguish the empanadas after they have been closed, I like to create a different seal for each filling. For the sausage and mushroom empanadas, press the back of a fork along the edges to seal the empanada. For the beef empanadas, pinch the edges together with your fingertips, then, starting at one end, create pleats by folding and pressing the edge of the empanada up and over onto itself.

{CONTINUED}

GLAZE AND GRILL THE EMPANADAS Place a grill topper on the grill grates. Heat your grill to medium (400°F) and close the lid. Wait at least 15 minutes before continuing.

Crack the egg into a small bowl and whisk lightly. Using a small paintbrush or basting brush, lightly brush the tops of the empanadas with the egg.

Oil the grill topper with a vegetable oil–soaked paper towel held with a long pair of tongs. Place the empanadas on the topper and close the grill lid. Allow the empanadas to cook for 12 minutes. Because the fillings are already fully cooked, the empanadas are ready when the dough is cooked and turns golden brown.

SERVE Transfer to a serving platter or basket and enjoy.

COOKING NOTES

INGREDIENTS

Commercial empanada dough You can purchase frozen empanada dough that comes in precut 5-inch circles. If you can find it, it's a good alternative to making your own. Simply defrost at room temperature before using.

Empanada dough is traditionally made with fresh lard. Because high-quality fresh lard is difficult to find, I use vegetable shortening, which still produces very good results.

TECHNIQUE

Finely diced beef The meat for the empanadas is traditionally chopped or diced; it is never ground. Ground beef releases too much liquid, resulting in a soggy empanada.

When chopping the meat, make sure the pieces are very small (less than ¼ inch) and all about the same size for even browning.

ADVANCE PREPARATION

The dough can be made a day in advance. Keep refrigerated and bring to room temperature before using.

Both fillings can also be made a day in advance.

The empanadas can be assembled and refrigerated a day in advance. If stacking uncooked empanadas, place a piece of parchment paper between each to keep them from sticking.

GRILLED ROSEMARY FLATBREAD

You only need to spend five minutes in Argentina to notice the influence that Italian culture has had on the country. And in no area is this more apparent than in its food. Pizzas and pastas are staples of the Argentine diet, as are red wine, provolone cheese, and small calzones (known in Argentina as empanadas). These grilled flatbreads partake of that heritage and are a popular starter at barbecues (*asados*). I love this nonyeasted bread dough for how quick and easy it is to make—and for how my guests are always impressed when I tell them I made it from scratch! **Serves 8**

3½ cups all-purpose flour
1 teaspoon baking powder
2 teaspoons salt
1 stick (½ cup) unsalted butter, cut into cubes, chilled
1 cup water
1 bunch fresh rosemary
1 cup olive oil
Fleur de sel or other crunchy finishing salt (optional)

PREPARE THE DOUGH Combine the flour, baking powder, and salt in the work bowl of a stand mixer or in a large mixing bowl and stir to combine. Scatter the butter pieces over the dry ingredients and, using your fingertips, squeeze the butter into the flour between your index finger and thumb until the butter pieces are the size of peas and evenly scattered throughout the flour.

Using the paddle attachment of your stand mixer, turn the machine on to medium-high speed and drizzle the water over the dry ingredients. Wait for the dough to come together into a ball. Continue mixing on medium-high for an additional 2 minutes (this step serves to knead the dough). Alternatively, use a handheld electric mixer at high speed for 3 minutes. Remove the dough from the bowl after it has formed a ball around the beaters, and on a floured work surface knead the dough by hand for 3 minutes.

COOKING NOTES

INGREDIENTS

Baking powder Because this dough is leavened with baking powder, it can be grilled as little as 30 minutes after it has been made (dough made with yeast needs more time).

TECHNIQUE

Shaping the dough You do not need a rolling pin to shape the dough. Simply place the dough on your work surface and, using your fingertips, push it out into a flat, circular shape, turning it in a circle as you do so.

ADVANCE PREPARATION

The dough can be made a day in advance, tightly wrapped in plastic, and refrigerated. Bring the dough to room temperature before rolling out and grilling.

Wrap the dough in plastic and allow to rest at room temperature for 30 minutes.

PREPARE THE ROSEMARY BRUSH Create a rosemary basting brush by tightly tying the rosemary stalks at their base with twine (or use a rubber band). Place the olive oil in a cup and set the rosemary brush tie side up in the oil.

{CONTINUED}

ROLL OUT THE DOUGH Cut the dough into 4 equal pieces. On a lightly floured work surface, use a rolling pin to roll out the dough into a 9-inch circle that is about ⅛ inch thick. Do not worry if the shape is irregular (I actually think it looks better that way). Set aside and repeat with the rest of the dough.

Using the rosemary brush, slather the tops of the rolled-out dough rounds with a coating of olive oil.

GRILL THE DOUGH AND SERVE Heat your grill to medium-high (450°F) and close the lid. Wait at least 15 minutes before continuing. Oil the grill grates with a vegetable oil–soaked paper towel held with a long pair of tongs.

Place the flatbreads, oiled side down, onto the grill grates and brush the tops of the dough with more oil. Close the grill lid and allow to cook for 3 to 4 minutes, until the crust develops grill marks and turns a golden brown color. Flip the flatbreads over, brush more oil on the tops, and allow to cook with the lid closed for an additional 3 to 4 minutes.

Remove the flatbreads from the grill and brush a bit more oil on top. If you like, while the bread is still hot you can sprinkle some finishing salt over it. Cut the bread into wedges as you would a pizza and serve warm.

ARUGULA-, GARLIC- & GREEN ONION– STUFFED FLANK STEAK {MATAMBRE}

If an Argentine offers you a *matambre*, I hope you are hungry. Traditionally, the dish, whose name literally translates to "hunger killer," is made up of a long piece of flank steak rolled around a stuffing of rice, beans, eggs, and anything else the cook decides to add. Just one slice has the makings of two meals! However, lighter variations do exist. My favorite is this one, stuffed with aromatic vegetables and leafy greens that work perfectly with the char-grilled flank steak. Try my combination, or use ingredients of your choice. **Serves 8**

8 cloves garlic
Salt
3 pounds flank steak, trimmed of excess fat
Black pepper
3 cups arugula leaves, washed and dried
1 bunch green onions, tops and roots trimmed,
    halved lengthwise then halved crosswise
3 tablespoons olive oil

PREPARE A GARLIC PASTE Prepare a garlic paste by mashing the garlic cloves with a teaspoon of salt in a mortar and pestle. If you do not have one, you can create one by smashing the garlic and salt inside a cup with the back of a wooden spoon. Otherwise, simply sprinkle the garlic with the salt and use your knife to chop it very finely by hand. In either case, you should end up with a wet garlic paste.

SEASON THE BEEF, ADD THE TOPPINGS, AND ROLL
Season the beef on both sides with salt and pepper and place lengthwise in front of you (the short sides of the rectangle should be parallel to you).

    Slather the garlic paste all over one side of the beef and top with the arugula and the green onions placed evenly across the surface of the meat. Drizzle the olive oil over the vegetables and season with more pepper.

    Starting with the short side closest to you, begin rolling the beef tightly, being careful to keep the arugula and green onions inside the roll. You

should end up with a tightly wound cylinder of flank steak. Place the beef roll seam side down on your work surface and cut three 18-inch pieces of cotton kitchen twine. Place them a few inches apart under the meat and wrap each tightly around the rolled beef and tie into a knot.

{CONTINUED}

GRILL AND SERVE Heat your grill to the highest setting and close the lid. Wait at least 15 minutes before continuing. Oil the grill grates with a vegetable oil–soaked paper towel held with a long pair of tongs.

Set the rolled meat on the grill seam side down and lower the lid. Cook for 8 minutes per side, rotating the roll twice (for a total cooking time of 24 minutes), until the internal temperature registers 125° to 130°F for medium-rare, or until it reaches the desired doneness (see chart on page 10).

Allow the meat to rest for 5 minutes on a work surface. Then cut off the twine and carve the roll into 1-inch-thick slices and arrange on a serving platter. If the steak was not long enough or if you did not tie the roll tight enough, it may fall apart when you slice it (I've had both happen to me). The steak and vegetables will still be delicious and can be attractively presented alongside each other on a platter.

COOKING NOTES

TECHNIQUES

Tying the meat So long as you use cotton twine (so it does not ignite) and are able to tie a knot, you will be able to do this. Use at least two—and preferably three—strings to keep the meat securely rolled as it cooks.

Taking an internal temperature When taking the internal temperature of the meat, be careful to keep the tip of thermometer probe inside the beef. Because the thin meat is rolled around vegetables, it is easy to accidentally take an incorrect measurement of the vegetables instead of the beef.

ADVANCE PREPARATION

The meat can be rolled and left refrigerated several hours before grilling. Bring the meat to room temperature before grilling.

FRESH PARSLEY SAUCE {CHIMICHURRI}

If you ask me, chimichurri is as tied to Argentina's national profile as gauchos and the tango. This incredibly versatile sauce, with its bright and vibrant flavors, can also be used as a grilling marinade for chicken, fish, or beef. Make extra to store as a flavorful addition to a midweek meal. **Makes 1¾ cups**

4 cloves garlic, peeled and crushed
1 teaspoon salt
2 cups lightly packed flat-leaf parsley leaves and
    tender stems, finely chopped
½ cup fresh oregano leaves, finely chopped
½ cup red wine vinegar
1 cup olive oil
1 tablespoon crushed red pepper

CREATE A GARLIC PASTE Place the crushed garlic on your cutting board and sprinkle the salt over it. Wait a minute or so; you will notice some moisture leaching from the garlic. Holding your knife blade almost parallel to the cutting board, scrape the blade over the chopped garlic a few times, turning the garlic into a semisoft paste. Place the garlic paste in a small mixing bowl.

COMBINE THE REMAINING INGREDIENTS Add the parsley, oregano, vinegar, oil, and crushed red pepper to the bowl with the garlic paste and stir until well combined.

SERVE OR STORE Place the sauce in a small serving bowl and serve. To store for later use, place in an airtight container and refrigerate.

COOKING NOTES

TECHNIQUE

Creating a garlic paste Garlic paste is made by mashing or scraping garlic cloves with salt, either with a mortar and pestle or on a cutting board with a knife. The salt is necessary to bring out the moisture in the garlic cloves. I use this technique often, especially when the garlic will be left raw, as it mellows the flavor a bit and eliminates the possibility that one of my guests or I will bite into a chunk of raw garlic.

ADVANCE PREPARATION

Chimichurri can be made in advance and kept in the refrigerator for up to 5 days.

CHAR-GRILLED VEGETABLES

Nothing is more inviting to me than a giant tray of colorful charred vegetables. I especially love carrots, since they have a good amount of natural sugars that caramelize beautifully on the grill. Choose your favorite seasonal veggies and leave them on the grill a bit longer than you normally would to truly char them and give their flavors a smoky dimension. **Serves 8**

3 carrots, peeled and cut lengthwise into quarters
1 bunch asparagus, ends trimmed
3 onions, peeled and cut through the root end
    into quarters
2 peppers, cored and cut into quarters
Olive oil
Salt and black pepper
2 lemons, halved

OIL AND SEASON THE VEGETABLES Place the carrots, asparagus, onions, and peppers in a large bowl, drizzle generously with olive oil, and season with salt and pepper.

GRILL THE VEGETABLES AND SERVE Heat your grill to medium-high (450°F) and close the lid. Wait at least 15 minutes before continuing.

Place all the vegetables on the grill, setting them crosswise on the grates so they do not fall between them. Place the lemons, cut side down, on the grill as well and close the lid.

Grill the vegetables until they develop grill marks and become charred in places, 4 to 6 minutes depending on how dense the vegetable is. The lemon will take a bit longer (but it does not need to be flipped). Turn the vegetables over and cook until the other side chars, again about 4 to 6 minutes. Remove the vegetables from the grill as they finish cooking and arrange on a serving platter.

Before serving, squeeze the grilled lemon halves over the charred vegetables.

COOKING NOTES

INGREDIENTS

Vegetables To make sure your vegetables char nicely but don't burn up and dry out, cut them on the larger side. This way they will maintain a firm, moist interior while the outside chars.

Lemon Grilling the lemon halves not only caramelizes the natural sugars found in the fruit, but it also loosens the citrus membranes, making the lemon extra juicy.

Because the acid in the lemon juice will turn the green vegetables a drab olive color, wait until you are ready to serve before squeezing the juice over the vegetables.

ADVANCE PREPARATION

The vegetables can be cut several hours in advance, but wait until you are ready to grill them before oiling and seasoning them. The vegetables can also be grilled a few hours in advance and served at room temperature. Remember not to squeeze the lemons over the vegetables until you are ready to serve.

SAVORY CORN PUDDING {HUMITA DE OLLA}

This dish from northern Argentina reminds me of summer creamed corn. It can be cooked in a pot (as it is here) or wrapped in corn husks and steamed (like a Mexican *tamal*). I love this version for its simplicity and deliciousness. There is something incredibly comforting about warm, creamy sweet corn, and when you pair it with charred grilled beef, you have a true winner! **Serves 8**

4½ cups corn (about 7 ears fresh or 32 ounces frozen corn, thawed)
¼ cup heavy cream
1 teaspoon cornstarch
2 tablespoons unsalted butter
1 tablespoon olive oil
1 onion, chopped (about 1 cup)
1 red pepper, cored and diced (about ¾ cup)
1 teaspoon salt
¼ teaspoon cayenne pepper
8 leaves basil

PUREE THE CORN Place the corn, heavy cream, and cornstarch in the jar of a blender or the work bowl of a food processor and puree until smooth. Set aside.

SAUTÉ THE VEGETABLES Heat a medium saucepan over medium heat and add the butter and oil. When the butter has melted completely, add the onion and red pepper and cook until the vegetables turn limp and translucent, about 6 minutes. Stir in the salt and cayenne pepper.

COOKING NOTES

TECHNIQUE

Pureeing the corn This dish is traditionally made by grating the corn off the cob. You can do that, but I opt for the quicker and easier method of pureeing the corn in a blender or food processor.

ADVANCE PREPARATION

This dish can be made up to a day in advance and kept in the refrigerator. Simply reheat before serving.

COOK THE CORN AND SERVE Add the corn mixture to the sautéed vegetables and cook over medium heat, stirring intermittently, until the corn is cooked, the mixture turns thick and creamy, and the flavors are blended, 10 to 12 minutes (frozen corn will take less time, about 8 minutes).

Remove the pot from the heat and allow the corn pudding to rest for 5 minutes; it will continue thickening.

Transfer to a serving bowl and garnish with the basil leaves.

DULCE de **LEUCE COOKIE CAKE**
{ALFAJOR GIGANTE}

Alfajores are to Argentina what Oreo cookies are to the United States. Found all over Argentina, they are made up of dulce de leche sandwiched between two cakey brown sugar cookies. The sandwich is then either dipped in chocolate or coated in confectioners' sugar. I love them so much that I decided to make a giant one! It's a great ending to any meal. Serve as you would a cake. **Serves 10**

2½ sticks (1¼ cups) unsalted butter, at room temperature
2 cups packed light brown sugar
3 eggs
1 tablespoon vanilla extract
2¼ cups all-purpose flour
1½ teaspoons baking powder
1½ teaspoons salt
1 cup dulce de leche, homemade (page 139) or store bought, or other caramel sauce
Confectioners' sugar, for dusting (about ¼ cup)

PREHEAT THE OVEN AND PREPARE CAKE PANS
Preheat the oven to 350°F. You will be using 2 oven racks, so make sure one is placed on the lower brackets and the other in the center.

Cut out parchment paper circles to fit in the bottoms of each of two 9-inch round cake pans (see Cooking Notes, right). Butter the bottoms of both pans, top with the parchment rounds, and butter the tops of the parchment rounds. Set aside.

MAKE THE BATTER Using a handheld electric mixer or stand mixer with the paddle attachment, beat the butter and sugar until smooth, about 2 minutes.

Add the eggs and vanilla and continue beating for another 3 minutes, until light and fluffy. If necessary, scrape the bottom of the bowl with a rubber spatula to fully incorporate all the ingredients.

COOKING NOTES

TECHNIQUE

Parchment rounds Parchment rounds are used to make it easier to remove a cake from its pan once it has cooled. Typically, they are only asked for if it would prove difficult to remove the cake without them. The easiest way to make them is to simply trace the bottom of the cake pan onto a piece of parchment and then cut it out with scissors, cutting a little bit inside the line you drew to account for the thickness of the pan's sides.

ADVANCE PREPARATION

You can make this cake a day in advance, but hold off on dusting it with the confectioners' sugar until just before you plan to serve it. Keep the cake wrapped in plastic at room temperature.

Place the flour, baking powder, and salt in a bowl and stir with a fork to combine. Add about a quarter of the flour mixture to the butter-sugar-egg mixture, beating until fully incorporated. Continue adding the flour in batches until it's all mixed in. The batter will be slightly thick. Be careful not to overbeat the mixture, as this will result in a tough cookie.

BAKE THE CAKE Pour half of the batter into each cake pan. Using a rubber spatula, carefully spread the batter toward all sides of the pan, making sure that the thickness of the batter is level throughout. This is necessary to ensure even cooking. Bake for 20 minutes, or until an inserted skewer or toothpick comes out clean.

COOL AND ASSEMBLE THE CAKE Remove the cakes from the oven and allow to cool for 15 minutes in the pans. Run a thin knife blade around the perimeter of the cakes and invert them onto a work surface. Peel off the parchment paper.

Place the cakes side by side with the bottoms (the sides you peeled the parchment off of) facing up. Spread the dulce de leche over the exposed surface of one of the cakes. Invert the plain cake over the one spread with dulce de leche, so that the sides of the cakes that had the parchment peeled off are the insides of the sandwich. Carefully move the cake onto a serving platter.

Dust a generous amount of confectioners' sugar over the top of the assembled cake. Slice and serve.

Chilean Seafood Cookout

Drink

White Wine Spritzers {160}

Starter

Bacon-Wrapped Scallops with
Charred Corn Salsa {160}

Main Courses

Wood Plank–Grilled Halibut /
Fletán a la Parrilla {162}

Grilled Clams & Chorizo /
Curanto al Disco {165}

Condiments & Sides

Chilean Hot Pepper Sauce /
Salsa Pebre {166}

Charred Potatoes and Pancetta {167}

Salad of Marinated Cheese,
Olives & Tomatoes {168}

Dessert

Meringue Cake with Dulce de
Leche & Berries / *Merengón con
Dulce de Leche y Bayas* {169}

Chilean cuisine is very much tied to Spain—you might even think of it as Spanish cuisine prepared with local Chilean ingredients and sprinkled with influences of other European countries such as Italy and Germany. Chile is a narrow, mountainous country (its average width is only 110 miles) with a very long coastline (over 2,600 miles). It is, understandably, a maritime-centric culture, and seafood is immensely popular. The country's mountainous terrain favors the breeding of smaller animals such as lamb, rabbit, and pig—rather than cattle—so these are the most common meats in the Chilean diet. Like their neighbors in Argentina, Chileans love to cook outdoors with wood and/or charcoal, and they make and drink a lot of wine. Corn, potatoes, garlic, and tomatoes are also important ingredients here at the southwestern edge of South America.

{MENU GAME PLAN}

One day in advance:

- Bake the meringue cake, but do not top it yet with berries and dulce de leche. Cover loosely. Storage: room temperature

The night before:

- Prepare the salad. Storage: refrigerator
- Prepare the hot pepper sauce. Storage: refrigerator

On the morning of:

- Soak the wooden plank for at least 2 hours.
- Wrap the scallops in bacon and cover. Storage: refrigerator
- Combine all the sauce ingredients for the clams and chorizo in a bowl. Storage: room temperature

Two to three hours before:

- Shuck the corn and soak it in water.
- Prepare the foil packets of pancetta and potatoes. Storage: room temperature
- Prepare the ingredients for charred corn salsa—except the corn—and combine them in a serving bowl. You'll grill and char the corn later. Storage: room temperature
- Finish dessert by topping the meringue with dulce de leche and berries. Storage: room temperature

In the hour before (setup):

- Set up the beverage bar with ingredients for the white wine spritzers.
- Set out:
  Salad of Marinated Cheese, Olives & Tomatoes
  Chilean Hot Pepper Sauce

As your event unfolds:

- Serve wine spritzers.
- Grill/char the corn and add to the salsa.
- Grill the bacon-wrapped scallops.
- Serve the starters.
- Roast and char the potato and pancetta packets.
- Place a pan on the grill and add the clam and chorizo sauce ingredients.
- Grill the chorizo and clams and add them to the sauce. Cover the pan with the pan lid or foil.
- Remove the wooden plank from the water and prepare it for grilling.
- Season the fish, place it on the plank, and grill.
- Serve the main courses.
- Serve dessert.

WHITE WINE SPRITZERS

This is a great starter for an outdoor cookout. Light and refreshing, it helps open your appetite while quenching your thirst. It's a great cocktail to serve in pitchers, and it looks fabulous in punch bowls. If you want to make individual spritzers, top a glass of white wine with some sparkling water and add a lemon wedge. **Serves 6**

1 bottle Chilean white wine, chilled
2½ cups sparkling water, chilled
2 lemons, sliced into rounds

Place all the ingredients in a glass pitcher and stir well. Serve in wine glasses and enjoy.

--- COOKING NOTES ---

INGREDIENTS

Chilean white wines The two most popular white wine varietals in Chile are chardonnay, which is fuller bodied, and sauvignon blanc, which is crisper. While both make good spritzers, I prefer using sauvignon blanc.

ADVANCE PREPARATION

It's best to serve the spritzers soon after you make them to preserve the effervescence of the sparkling water.

BACON-WRAPPED SCALLOPS with Charred Corn Salsa

When I first tasted this dish, I knew it would be a keeper. All of its delicious elements make it the perfect starter salad: sweet, smoky meat set over a tangy salsa of tomato, basil, and charred corn. This colorful dish, which can be left out at room temperature with little effect on its taste or texture, is also great to serve on its own as a light lunch. **Serves 8**

4 ears fresh corn, husks on but silks removed
    (see page 33)
1 pint cherry tomatoes, quartered
Leaves from 3 or 4 stems fresh basil (about
    20 leaves), cut into thin strips
2 green onions, white parts only, sliced thin
Juice of 1 lemon
2 tablespoons olive oil
Salt and black pepper
8 large sea scallops (about 1 pound total)
4 strips bacon, cut in half crosswise

SOAK THE CORN Place the corn in a large stockpot or other container large enough to hold all the ears, and fill it with water. If you do not have a sufficiently large container, use your kitchen sink.

Allow the corn to soak for 20 minutes. Remove from the water, shake, and tightly squeeze the husks against the kernels of corn to remove excess water.

GRILL THE CORN Heat your grill to high (550°F) and close the lid. Wait at least 15 minutes before lowering the heat to medium-high (450°F) and continuing. Oil the grill grates with a vegetable oil–soaked paper towel held with a long pair of tongs.

Place the corn on the rack, close the lid, and grill for 5 minutes. Turn the corn over and grill for another 5 minutes. Remove from the grill.

PULL OFF THE HUSKS AND CHAR THE CORN Increase the grill temperature to high. Pull off the husks from the cobs of corn and discard them. Place the cobs directly on the grill and close the lid. Allow the kernels to char for about 5 minutes per side, or until they become dark and golden brown on all sides. Remove from the grill and set aside. Close the grill lid to keep the grill temperature up; you'll be grilling the scallops next.

PREPARE THE SALAD On a work surface, slice the corn kernels from the cobs with a sharp knife. Collect all the kernels and place them in a mixing bowl. Add the tomatoes, basil, and green onions to the bowl and toss well. Drizzle in the lemon juice and olive oil and season with salt and pepper. Mix well. Taste and adjust seasoning if necessary.

PREPARE AND GRILL THE SCALLOPS Season each scallop with salt and pepper. Wrap a slice of bacon around each, covering the scallop's flat sides.

Oil the grill grates with a vegetable oil–soaked paper towel held with a long pair of tongs. Place the scallops on the grill, making sure to set the bacon seam side down, and lower the heat to medium-high. Close the lid and grill for 6 minutes. Turn the scallops over and grill for another 6 minutes.

SERVE Spoon the salad onto a large serving platter, top with the scallops, and serve.

COOKING NOTES

TECHNIQUES

Basil strips Slicing basil into thin strips, called *chiffonade,* is very easy to do. Simply stack the basil leaves on top of each other and then roll them into a cylinder like a cigarette. Use your knife to slice the leaves crosswise into thin strips. Shake the strips loose from each other.

Wrapping scallops in bacon Wrapping lean cuts of meat with fat in order to prevent the meat from drying out is called *barding.* In this recipe, bacon not only keeps the scallops moist, it also infuses the shellfish with its smoky flavor.

ADVANCE PREPARATION

The salad can be made a few hours in advance. The scallops can be grilled a couple of hours in advance and kept at room temperature before serving.

WOOD PLANK–GRILLED HALIBUT
{FLETÁN A LA PARRILLA}

I love grilled fish, but I don't always love the care needed to make sure it doesn't dry out. Even the fattiest of fish can become desiccated and tasteless if cooked improperly. My solution is to grill fish on wood grilling planks. Not only do they protect the fish's moisture by allowing the fish to sit in its own juices, they impart a beautiful smoky flavor and deep, rich color reminiscent of the wood-burning grills of the Southern Cone. Once you see how easy the planks are to work with (and how quick cleanup becomes), I am sure you will keep a supply of them around. **Serves 8**

2½ to 3 pounds halibut fillet (one large fillet or a
    few smaller ones)
Olive oil
Salt and pepper

COOKING NOTES

INGREDIENTS

Halibut Halibut can be purchased as fillets or steaks, and either would work well in this recipe. This lean, firm, white-fleshed fish has a very mild flavor and is available year-round. While the halibut's dense meatiness makes it a great grilling fish, it's best to use a wood plank when grilling to keep the lean flesh from drying out.

TECHNIQUE

Wood grilling planks I love grilling fish on thin wooden planks, because I don't have to worry about my fish sticking to or falling in between the grates, and cleanup is a snap. The planks won't give you grill marks, but they will give you moist, smoky fish with a deep tan color. The planks come in different types of wood, but cedar, which gives off a mild smoky flavor, is the most popular.

Found at kitchenware stores as well as many food markets, the planks are disposable, so you can simply discard them after you are done using them.

ADVANCE PREPARATION

The wooden plank should be soaked at least 2 hours in advance. However, the fish should be seasoned and grilled right before serving.

SOAK THE WOOD PLANK Soak a plank in water for 2 hours. (I put mine in the kitchen sink and place a pot over it to keep it submerged.)

PREPARE THE PLANK FOR GRILLING Heat your grill to high (550°F) and close the lid. Wait at least 15 minutes before continuing.

Using tongs or a heat-proof grill glove, place your soaked plank on the grill for 2 minutes, then turn the board over and grill for another 2 minutes. Repeat, so that you will have grilled each side for a total of 4 minutes. You will hear the wood snap. The snapping sounds will continue throughout the grilling process. Leave the plank on the grill while you season your fish.

SEASON AND GRILL THE FISH Drizzle olive oil on both sides of the fish and then season each side with salt and pepper. Place the fish directly on the wood plank and close the grill lid.

After a few minutes you should begin to see smoke come out the sides of the grill. Cook for 15 minutes, or until the fish is cooked through. If the fillets are less than 1 inch thick, begin checking for doneness after 12 minutes. You know it is ready when the flesh begins to flake and separate, and when a metal skewer inserted into the flesh feels warm to the touch when removed.

SERVE For an attractively rustic presentation, serve the fish directly on the wooden plank.

GRILLED CLAMS & CHORIZO {CURANTO AL DISCO}

I like to think of this dish as a Latin clambake. A smoked paprika and butter sauce serves as the base to which grilled chorizo and grilled clams are added. It's quick, easy, and delicious! If you have never grilled clams, you will see just how quickly they cook and how flavorful they are. But the best part is that, since you can see them pop open, you won't have to worry about the clams overcooking and turning rubbery. This recipe is as fun to make as it is delicious to eat. **Serves 8**

1½ pounds fresh chorizo
1 stick (½ cup) unsalted butter, diced
1½ cups white wine
4 cloves garlic, minced
3 shallots, sliced
2 tomatoes, chopped
1½ teaspoons smoked paprika
Salt and black pepper
36 small clams in the shell, scrubbed
Extra-virgin olive oil
1 baguette, halved lengthwise
¼ cup lightly packed flat-leaf parsley leaves and
     tender stems, chopped
3 lemons, cut into wedges

GRILL THE CHORIZO AND PREPARE THE SAUCE
Heat your grill to medium-high (450°F) and close the lid. Wait at least 15 minutes before continuing. Oil the grill grates with a vegetable oil–soaked paper towel held with a long pair of tongs.

Place the chorizo on one side of the grill, close the lid, and cook for 8 to 10 minutes, or until the chorizo is a deep golden brown. Turn the sausage over and grill for another 4 to 5 minutes, until its skin is charred and shriveled. Remove the chorizo from the grill.

Set a roasting pan set on the other side of the grill and add the butter, wine, garlic, shallots, tomatoes, smoked paprika, ½ teaspoon of salt, and ¼ teaspoon of black pepper. Cook, stirring inter-mittently, for 8 minutes, or until the tomatoes start to break down and the shallots soften.

COOKING NOTES

INGREDIENTS

Clams Use your favorite clams in this recipe, or feel free to experiment with different types of shellfish, such as mussels. Shrimp also work really well in this recipe.

EQUIPMENT

I have used everything from a stainless-steel roasting pan to a paella pan to a disposable foil roasting pan—all with success. Just make sure the pan fits on the grill with enough extra space to grill the chorizo and clams.

ADVANCE PREPARATION

All of the ingredients for the sauce can be prepared and placed in the pan. As the clams can become rubbery as they sit, the clams and chorizo should be grilled just before serving.

Meanwhile, slice the chorizo into thin rounds and add to the pan with the sauce. Stir to combine, and leave the pan on the grill.

GRILL THE CLAMS Increase the grill heat to high (550°F), leaving the lid open.

Place the clams directly on the grill grate and cook until they pop open, about 3 to 6 minutes. Use tongs to transfer the clams to the pan as soon as they open. Discard any clams that remain shut after 8 or 9 minutes.

{CONTINUED}

Toss the clams, chorizo, and sauce together, and set aside.

GRILL AND SLICE THE BREAD Drizzle some olive oil over the inside of the cut baguette and place the bread halves cut side down on the grill. Allow to toast for a few minutes, until slightly charred and toasted. Remove from the heat and cut into slices.

SERVE Garnish the clams and chorizo with a sprinkling of parsley and wedges of lemon. Serve with the baguette slices.

CHILEAN HOT PEPPER SALSA {SALSA PEBRE}

Think of this sauce as a cross between a fresh herb- and oil-based Argentine chimichurri and a hot, chunky Mexican salsa. Chile's shared border with Argentina explains half of it, and while Chile is not geographically close to Mexico, it is close to Peru, where hot, chile-tinged sauces are commonly used. This classic Chilean sauce is a great accompaniment to grilled meats, seafood, and vegetables, and it works wonderfully as a spicy spread on sandwiches. In this menu, it accompanies the wood plank–grilled fish. **Makes about ¾ cup**

¼ cup plus 2 tablespoons red wine vinegar
5 cloves garlic, peeled
6 green onions, roots and tops trimmed
1 or 2 serrano chiles, stemmed
2 cups lightly packed cilantro leaves and tender stems, chopped
2 plum tomatoes, cored and chopped
¼ cup plus 1 tablespoon extra-virgin olive oil
1 teaspoon salt

PUREE THE AROMATIC INGREDIENTS Place the red wine vinegar, garlic, green onions, and chile in a blender or small food processor. Puree until smooth.

MIX IN THE REMAINING INGREDIENTS Pour the pureed mixture into a bowl and blend in the cilantro, tomatoes, olive oil, and salt. Serve or set aside for up to a day.

CHARRED POTATOES & PANCETTA

Chapaleles, deep-fried potato cakes flavored with pork rinds, are commonly served in Chile as a side dish or snack. This recipe finds inspiration from the chapalele, but simplifies the preparation by roasting potatoes and pancetta together in a foil packet on the grill. The results are pancetta-perfumed Yukon gold potatoes that are crispy and charred on the outside and moist and pillowy on the inside. **Serves 8**

3 pounds Yukon gold potatoes, scrubbed and cut into small wedges
½ pound pancetta, diced
4 shallots, peeled and cut into quarters through the root end
4 sprigs fresh thyme, plus more for garnish
½ cup olive oil
Salt and black pepper

PREPARE FOIL PACKETS Cut a piece of foil about 14 inches in length and place ¼ of the potatoes, ¼ of the pancetta, and 4 quarters of a shallot in its center. Sprinkle the leaves of one sprig of thyme over the vegetables and drizzle with 2 tablespoons of olive oil. Season with salt and pepper and toss the vegetables gently with your hands to coat them in oil and seasonings.

Seal the packet by bringing the long sides of the foil up toward the center and folding the edges over a couple of times to create a seal. Bring the ends up towards the center and seal by crimping the foil shut. Repeat the process three times to end up with a total of 4 packets.

ROAST THE PACKETS Heat your grill to high (550°F) and close the lid. Wait at least 15 minutes before lowering the heat to medium-high (450°F) and continuing.

Place the potato packets on the grill shelf and close the lid. If you do not have a grill shelf, lower the heat to medium and place the packets directly on the grates. Allow the potatoes to roast for 40 minutes,

or until tender. I test this by skewering the tip of a thin knife through the foil and into a potato. If I don't meet resistance, the potatoes are ready.

{CONTINUED}

COOKING NOTES

INGREDIENTS

Yukon gold potatoes Developed in Canada, Yukon golds are among the most versatile potatoes. They have a richly flavored yellow flesh, which many say has a buttery taste. A good substitute for them in this recipe is small red potatoes.

Pancetta Pancetta is pork belly that has been salt cured and flavored with spices but is not smoked. It is typically found rolled. Simply eliminate it if you cannot find pancetta, as it is difficult to find a suitable substitute for it in this recipe.

TECHNIQUE

Removing thyme leaves Pinch the top of the sprig with your thumb and index finger and gently pull down towards the bottom of the sprig, going against the growth of the leaves. The leaves will come right off. The thin, soft stems that come off with the leaves are fine to leave in.

ADVANCE PREPARATION

The packets can be prepared a few hours in advance and left at room temperature. The packets can also be roasted in the oven (at 450°F for 30 minutes) until you are ready to char them on the grill.

CHAR THE POTATOES Increase the grill heat to high (550°F). Place the packets directly on the grates, close the lid, and allow to cook for 15 minutes to char the bottom of the potatoes. Open the packets, being careful not to burn yourself with the steam, and transfer the potatoes to a serving bowl. You may need to peel off some of the potatoes that have become stuck and charred to the foil. (If the potatoes have not developed a charred crust, close the foil packet and return to the grill until they do.) Remove the packets from the grill and set aside.

GARNISH AND SERVE Transfer to a serving bowl and garnish with some fresh sprigs of thyme.

SALAD of MARINATED CHEESE, OLIVES & TOMATOES

While this very easy side dish is great to serve year-round, I especially love to make it when tomatoes are at their peak. I use cherry or grape tomatoes here since they are usually in good condition even when the other tomatoes are pale and lifeless. But if you can gather tomatoes in a variety of shapes and colors and throw them into the mix, you will take this salad to another level. **Serves 8**

10 ounces manchego cheese, cubed
½ cup olive oil
¼ cup red wine vinegar
Leaves from 4 sprigs of thyme
1 cup pitted olives
3 green onions, white parts only, sliced thin
1 pint cherry or grape tomatoes, halved
Salt and black pepper
1 head romaine lettuce, leaves torn by hand

MARINATE THE CHEESE, OLIVES, AND TOMATOES
Place cheese, olive oil, vinegar, thyme leaves, olives, green onions, and tomatoes in a mixing bowl and toss well. Season with salt and pepper and allow the mixture to marinate at room temperature for 2 hours.

ASSEMBLE THE SALAD Place the lettuce leaves on a large platter. Top with the cheese, olives, tomatoes, and all their marinade, toss well, and serve.

COOKING NOTES

INGREDIENTS

Manchego cheese This semifirm sheep's milk cheese has a slightly sharp flavor. It is made in 10-inch round wheels that have a recognizable zigzag pattern embossed on the rind; the rounds are typically cut into wedges that are wrapped for sale.

You can use a different cheese in this recipe; just make sure it is not a soft cheese, which will fall apart in the marinade.

ADVANCE PREPARATION

The marinated cheese, olive, and tomato mixture gets better with time. If you can, prepare it a day in advance, keep it refrigerated, and bring out to come to room temperature 2 hours before serving.

MERINGUE CAKE with Dulce de Leche & Berries
{MERENGÓN CON DULCE DE LECHE Y BAYAS}

Inspired by the classic New Zealand dessert, the pavlova, this recipe uses a slow-baked meringue as a base for mixed berries. But because dessert in this part of the world is not complete without the addition of dulce de leche, I made sure to slather a thin layer of it between the meringue and the fruit. **Serves 8 to 10**

1½ cups confectioners' sugar, plus more for garnish
¼ cup packed brown sugar
1 teaspoon cornstarch
2 teaspoons vanilla extract
2 teaspoons distilled white vinegar
6 egg whites
1½ cups dulce de leche
1 pint raspberries
½ pint blueberries
½ pint blackberries

PREPARE A BAKING SHEET Set a rack in the center of the oven and preheat to 350°F. Line a baking sheet with parchment paper. Set aside.

PREPARE THE MERINGUE Place the confectioners' sugar, brown sugar, and cornstarch in a bowl and mix well, making sure to break up any clumps of brown sugar. Set aside.

In a small bowl, combine the vanilla extract and vinegar and set aside.

Using a stand mixer with the paddle attachment or a handheld electric mixer, whip the egg whites on high until frothy. Lower the speed to medium and add the sugar mixture about ½ cup at a time, incorporating each addition before adding more sugar. Add the vanilla-vinegar mixture and whip for another minute, until the egg whites have a glossy sheen to them and form soft peaks.

Using a rubber spatula, scoop the meringue into the center of the parchment-lined baking sheet and spread it into a circle. It is not important that the circle be perfectly round, but try to make it about 9 inches across and 2 inches tall. Level the top so that the meringue cooks evenly.

COOKING NOTES

TECHNIQUE

Adding vinegar to the meringue Vinegar (or another acid) is added to meringue to prevent overbeating, which could cause the meringue to become lumpy or collapse. The vinegar does not change the meringue's flavor.

ADVANCE PREPARATION

This dessert can be assembled several hours in advance. You can prepare the meringue the night before and add the dulce de leche and fruit a few hours before serving. Wait until you are ready to serve before dusting the cake with confectioner's sugar.

BAKE THE MERINGUE Lower the oven to 275°F and bake the meringue for 1½ hours, or until it has turned a tan color and the top has hardened and begun to crack. Turn off the heat and allow the meringue to cool in the oven for 1 hour.

ASSEMBLE THE DESSERT AND SERVE Remove the meringue from the parchment and place it top side up on a serving dish. The meringue is very light, and will seem as if it may crack, but it is sturdier than you think. If it does crack, don't worry about it; it will be covered with dulce de leche.

Spread the dulce de leche all over the top of the meringue and cover with the berries. Garnish the top of the dessert with a dusting of confectioners' sugar. Serve and enjoy.

Brazilian Rodizio

Drink

Caipiroska {172}

Starter

Grilled Salad {172}

Sugarcane-Skewered Shrimp with
Coconut-Lime Glaze {175}

Main Courses

Charcoal-Grilled Skewers of Steak,
Sausage & Chicken / *Churrascada* {177}

Condiments & Sides

Smoked Paprika Oil {179}

Hot Pepper & Lime Sauce {180}

Yuca Soufflé / *Suflé de Yuca* {181}

Black Bean, Bacon & Rice Salad {183}

Dessert

Coconut Cupcakes {184}

Brazilian gastronomy is a combination of the many cultures that make up the country. But the three groups that have had the biggest impact on Brazil's cuisine are the native peoples, the conquering Portuguese, and the African slaves who were brought to work on the sugarcane plantations—and who had a huge impact on Brazilian cooking by turning peppers, coconut, and leafy greens into Brazilian staples. These groups all brought to the table their own culinary techniques, which they put to use with local ingredients. The "cowboy" cuisine that is popular in Argentina is also popular in Brazil: Brazilians love beef and pork cooked over charcoal. Aromatics like garlic and parsley, manioc (also known as cassava or yuca), rice, and black beans are also central to Brazilian cuisine.

{MENU GAME PLAN}

One day in advance:

- Prepare the cupcakes and cover them with plastic wrap. Do not prepare the meringue yet. Storage: room temperature

The night before:

- Prepare the coconut-lime glaze. Storage: refrigerator
- Prepare the Smoked Paprika Oil. Storage: room temperature
- Prepare the Hot Pepper & Lime Sauce. Storage: refrigerator

On the morning of:

- Prepare the Black Bean, Bacon & Rice Salad. Cover with a damp towel. Storage: room temperature
- Prepare the sugarcane skewers (if using) or soak some wooden skewers.
- Prepare the meringue and spread it on the cupcakes. Toast the coconut flakes and sprinkle over the meringue. Storage: room temperature

Two to three hours before:

- Bake the Yuca Soufflé. Storage: room temperature
- Skewer the shrimp. Storage: refrigerator
- Skewer the meats onto metal skewers. Storage: refrigerator
- Prepare foil packets of tomatoes for the grilled salad. Storage: room temperature

In the hour before (setup):

- Set up the bar with ingredients for the Caipiroskas.
- Put the Yuca Soufflé in the oven.
- Cut the lettuce and lemons for the grilled salad. Cover with a damp towel. Storage: room temperature
- Set out:
  Black Bean, Bacon & Rice Salad (keep covered with a damp towel)
  Smoked Paprika Oil
  Hot Pepper & Lime Sauce

As your event unfolds:

- Prepare and serve the Caipiroskas.
- Glaze and grill the shrimp skewers.
- Serve the starters.
- Salt and grill the meats.
- Grill the salad ingredients.
- Serve the main courses and sides.
- Serve dessert.

CAIPIROSKA

Brazil is known for its Caipirinha, a cocktail made with cachaça (a sugarcane liquor), lime, and sugar. However, the Caipiroska, a similar cocktail made with vodka, is also quite popular. I made a pitcher of these for a party when I only had vodka in the house and they now hold a permanent place in my cocktail repertoire. **Makes 1 cocktail**

1 lime, cut into 8 wedges
1 teaspoon sugar
2 ounces vodka
Ice

Place the lime wedges and sugar in a short rocks glass. Use a muddler or the handle of a wooden spoon to mash the lime and sugar until you have extracted all the juice from the fruit and the sugar has dissolved. Pour in the vodka, top with ice, and stir.

─── COOKING NOTES ───

ADVANCE PREPARATION

The recipe can easily be multiplied and left to chill in the refrigerator.

To make a party pitcher for 8:
8 limes, cut into small wedges
2 tablespoons plus 2 teaspoons sugar
16 ounces vodka

When you're ready to serve, fill short rocks glasses with ice and pour 2 ounces of the sweet-and-sour vodka into each glass. Scoop out some of the crushed lime wedges into each glass.

GRILLED SALAD

I love the cooked leafy green vegetables, such as collard greens and kale, that are served as side dishes in Brazil. So I wanted to keep the idea of serving wilted greens while still maintaining the freshness of a green salad. I came up with this grilled salad, and it has become my go-to summer salad. **Serves 8 to 10**

1 pint cherry or grape tomatoes, stemmed
Olive oil
Salt and black pepper
1 lemon, halved
1 lime, halved
3 hearts of romaine lettuce, split in half lengthwise

PREPARE THE TOMATO PACKETS Cut 2 pieces of foil about 14 inches in length. Place half of the tomatoes in the center of each piece of foil, drizzle with olive oil, and season with salt and pepper.

Seal the packets by bringing the long sides of the foil up towards the center and folding the edges over a couple of times to create a seal. Bring the ends up towards the center and crimp the foil shut.

GRILL THE TOMATO PACKETS AND CITRUS FRUIT
Heat your grill to high (550°F) and close the lid.
Wait at least 15 minutes before lowering the heat to
medium-high (450°F) and continuing.

Place the tomato packets on the grill. Place the
lemon and lime halves cut side down on the grill.
Close the lid and allow to cook for 5 minutes.

GRILL THE LETTUCE Oil the grill grates with a vegetable oil–soaked paper towel held with a long pair
of tongs. Drizzle olive oil over the cut sides of the
romaine hearts and season with salt and pepper.
Open the grill lid and place the lettuces cut side
down on the grill. Cook all the vegetables with the
lid open for about 3 minutes, or until the lettuce
develops grill marks.

SERVE Remove the tomato packets from the grill
and open them carefully to protect yourself from
hot steam escaping. Place the romaine hearts on a
platter and pour the tomatoes over them. Squeeze
the lemon and lime halves over all and serve
immediately.

COOKING NOTES

TECHNIQUE

Caramelizing citrus fruit Citrus fruits have
natural sugars that caramelize when heated, inten-
sifying the bright flavors of the fruit. Grilling halved
citrus fruits cut side down allows this process to
occur.

ADVANCE PREPARATION

You can prepare the tomato packets a few
hours before you plan on grilling them. Otherwise this should be prepared immediately before
serving.

SUGARCANE-SKEWERED SHRIMP with Coconut-Lime Glaze

I love to start a cookout with skewers of shrimp. Because these meaty morsels cook in less than 8 minutes, you can offer your guests a freshly grilled appetizer in no time. The fresh sugarcane serves as an unexpected spear, while the glaze is perfectly balanced between sweet coconut and tart lime. Small skewers that measure about 5 inches long and hold 2 shrimp make the perfect appetizer serving. **Serves 8**

Coconut-Lime Glaze
1½ cups coconut milk
¾ cup cream of coconut
¾ cup lime juice (from 6 to 8 limes)
¼ teaspoon cayenne pepper
½ teaspoon salt

3 pounds large shrimp, peeled and deveined
16 (5-inch) sugarcane skewers
Salt and black pepper
3 limes, cut into wedges

PREPARE THE GLAZE Place all the glaze ingredients in a medium saucepan and bring to a boil over medium-high heat (make sure you have enough space in the top of the pot as the mixture will bubble). Lower the heat to medium and cook for 25 minutes, or until the mixture is reduced by two-thirds. It will take on a dark tan color. Stir intermittently to prevent the mixture from sticking to the bottom of the pot. Set aside.

{CONTINUED ON NEXT PAGE}

COOKING NOTES

INGREDIENTS

Sugarcane This hard, fibrous grass has an inedible skin that must be peeled off before the moist beige flesh can be chewed (though even the sweet, tough flesh is not swallowed). See below for how to make sugarcane skewers. If you cannot find sugarcane, substitute small wooden or metal skewers, making sure to soak the wooden ones thoroughly before using.

Coconut milk Coconut milk is a liquid made by simmering shredded coconut in an equal amount of water and then straining it. For best results, use the full-fat variety of coconut milk—the low-fat kind has a much milder flavor.

Cream of coconut This is a commercially produced canned condiment made of sweetened coconut cream. Coconut cream, which is thicker than coconut milk, is made by simmering four parts shredded coconut with one part water and then straining it. Cream of coconut is one of the main ingredients in piña coladas.

TECHNIQUE

Making sugarcane skewers While you may be able to find sugarcane that is trimmed and ready to use as skewers, you may only find a whole piece of fresh sugarcane to work with. To convert the cane to skewers, first cut it crosswise into 9-inch-long pieces using a large, sharp chef's knife. Then cut each piece lengthwise in half, and then in half again or in thirds to create 4 or 6 long, wedge-shaped pieces. Finally, use a paring knife to trim one end of each skewer into a sharp point.

ADVANCE PREPARATION

The coconut glaze can be made a few hours in advance; it can stay out at room temperature for a few hours or kept in the refrigerator. If refrigerated, bring the glaze to room temperature before using. The shrimp can be skewered, left unseasoned, and kept refrigerated a few hours in advance.

PREPARE THE SHRIMP Skewer about 2 shrimp onto each sugarcane spear. If the skewers aren't sharp enough you may need to make small incisions through the shrimp with a thin knife.

GLAZE AND GRILL THE SHRIMP Heat your grill to high (550°F) and close the lid. Wait at least 15 minutes before continuing.

Season the shrimp all over with salt and pepper and slather glaze over all sides as well.

Oil the grill grates with a vegetable oil–soaked paper towel held with a long pair of tongs.

Place the shrimp skewers on the grill and keep the lid open so the shrimp don't overcook before the sugars in the glaze caramelize.

Grill the shrimp for about 4 minutes per side, basting as it cooks with more glaze. The shrimp are ready when they turn opaque and the glaze begins to caramelize.

SERVE Arrange the shrimp skewers on a platter and serve with lime wedges to squeeze over the shrimp.

CHARCOAL-GRILLED SKEWERS OF STEAK, SAUSAGE & CHICKEN {CHURRASCADA}

I have to say that one of my favorite culinary aromas is that of charcoal burning in a grill. And while I am often guilty of turning to the convenience of the gas grill, when I have a bit more time I like to bring out the charcoal and grill over fire. The added effort is minimal in comparison to the added "oomph" you will get—and this is one recipe where charcoal makes a real difference.

In Brazil, an invitation to a *churrascada* is an invitation to a grilling feast, where it is very common to have charcoal-grilled meat seasoned only with rock salt. Traditionally, the cut of beef that is served is the *picanha* (pee-KAHN-yah). The exact cut is not available in the U.S., but it is similar to top sirloin. These 2-inch boneless steaks are curled into a letter C formation and speared onto large metal skewers, as you would do to shrimp, which is said to keep the meat moist. The salt perfectly seasons the meat, allowing its pure flavors to stand out. I was apprehensive the first time I tried this super-simple technique, but now I'm a convert.

If you are making this recipe as part of a whole menu in which you'll be grilling other foods on your gas grill, it's fine to go with gas here too. **Serves 8**

1 pound hanger steak
1 pound beef sirloin
1 pound boneless, skinless chicken breasts
1 pound fresh chorizo
Rock salt

PREPARE THE CHARCOAL GRILL Light your charcoal and wait for about 80 percent of the coals to ash before spreading them out evenly over your lower grate. Spread a light coating of vegetable oil over your top grate and set it in place.

SKEWER THE MEAT In the meantime, prepare your meat. Cut the hanger steak and sirloin crosswise into 2-inch chunks. Slice the chicken breasts into large chunks and leave the chorizo whole. Skewer the beef, chicken, and chorizo onto large metal skewers.

SEASON AND GRILL THE MEAT Season the hanger steak, sirloin, and chicken liberally with rock salt by sprinkling the salt over the meat and then patting it in with your hands. Place the skewers on the grate and grill until the chicken and chorizo are cooked

{CONTINUED}

COOKING NOTES

INGREDIENTS

Rock salt This salt comes in chunky crystals that are typically placed in salt grinders. Make sure to use the natural, food-grade variety and not the one used for salting driveways or for making ice cream, as those salt crystals contain impurities.

Do not be alarmed by the size of the salt crystals. It may seem as if you are oversalting, but you are not. The crystals are so large that they will not completely dissolve and will eventually fall off the meat.

ADVANCE PREPARATION

The meat can be cut and skewered a couple of hours in advance and left refrigerated. Bring to room temperature before grilling. Do not season with salt until ready to grill.

through; this will depend on the intensity of the heat from the charcoal but should take about 20 to 25 minutes. Grill the hanger steak and sirloin until it reaches the desired doneness (see chart on page 10).

REST THE MEAT THEN SERVE Remove the cooked meats from the grill and allow to rest for 5 minutes before serving. Place the skewers on a large serving platter or big wooden cutting board and allow your guests to slice off their meat.

SMOKED PAPRIKA OIL

This is a great oil to drizzle on grilled vegetables and meats, as it imparts a smoky flavor while adding a touch of moistness. It's an easy and quick way to perk up your grilled dishes. A little goes a long way and, if you are lucky enough to have some left over, it will keep for a few weeks. **Makes ½ cup**

½ cup grape seed oil or other neutral oil
1 tablespoon smoked paprika

INFUSE THE OIL Place the oil in a small saucepan and set over very low heat. Add the paprika and stir. Allow the mixture to sit over the heat for 15 minutes.

Turn off the heat and allow the oil mixture to sit in the pan for 1 hour.

STRAIN THE OIL Place a coffee filter over the top of a glass. Flip the top of the filter over the lip of the glass so that the filter stays secure atop the glass. Pour the oil into the filter, being careful not to allow the oil to overflow.

Allow the oil to strain through the filter. This will be a slow process, taking about 20 minutes. Transfer the strained oil to a bowl or a squeeze bottle for serving. To use, pass the oil around the table and drizzle on the meat as a condiment.

COOKING NOTES

INGREDIENTS

Grape seed oil When preparing an infused oil, it is crucial to use a neutral oil that imparts no flavor of its own, which would cloud the essence of the spice. Grape seed oil, which is extracted from the seeds of wine grapes, is one of the most neutral and clean-tasting oils.

TECHNIQUE

Infusing oil This technique can be used with other spices such as curry or chile powder.

ADVANCE PREPARATION

The oil can be made well in advance and stored in an airtight container or bottle for up to 2 to 3 weeks at room temperature.

HOT PEPPER & LIME SAUCE
{MOLHO DE PIMIENTA E LIMÃO}

This salsalike raw sauce, *molho de pimienta e limão*, is a staple condiment in Brazil and is always served with grilled meats. Its kick of heat plays against the tang of the lime juice. So simple yet so intense! **Makes about 1½ cups**

1 clove garlic, peeled and crushed
½ teaspoon salt
4 to 6 malagueta peppers, stemmed and chopped
½ onion, very finely chopped (½ cup)
½ cup lime juice (from 4 or 5 limes)

CREATE A GARLIC PASTE Place the crushed garlic clove on your cutting board and sprinkle the salt over it. Wait a minute or so until the garlic releases some moisture. Holding your knife blade almost parallel to the cutting board, scrape the blade over the chopped garlic. Repeat this motion a few times until the garlic has become a semisoft paste. Place the garlic paste in a small mixing bowl.

COMBINE ALL THE INGREDIENTS AND SERVE Place all the remaining ingredients in the bowl with the garlic and combine well. Serve and enjoy.

COOKING NOTES

INGREDIENTS

Malagueta peppers These very small, spicy red chiles are often found packed in a bottle of vinegar. They are available in Latin markets or online. Suitable substitutes are Tabasco peppers, which are also sold bottled in vinegar; bird or Thai chiles; or serrano chiles. In the case of the latter two, use only one or two chiles, as they are considerably hotter than malaguetas.

ADVANCE PREPARATION

This sauce can be made in advance and kept refrigerated for up to 4 days. After that the lime may begin to take on a bitter flavor.

YUCA SOUFFLÉ {SUFLÉ DE YUCA}

Don't let the word souffle scare you. While this is made using the traditional souffle method, it is served as a fallen souffle, which means there is no stress involved in making sure it gets served in time. What you do get is a light and fluffy dish of yuca (cassava) that captures the tuber's sweet, nutty flavor. As is the case with most root vegetable side dishes, this goes with almost anything. It's become my new alternative to rice. **Serves 8**

1 pound yuca, peeled and diced
½ stick (¼ cup) unsalted butter, plus more for
    greasing the pan, at room temperature
Salt
½ cup milk, at room temperature
4 eggs, separated

BOIL THE YUCA Place the yuca in a pot of salted boiling water and cook until fork tender, about 20 minutes. The boiling liquid will have thickened and turned slightly opaque. Drain the yuca and place it in a large mixing bowl.

PREHEAT THE OVEN AND PREPARE THE PAN Preheat the oven to 350°F. Grease a 9-inch round or square baking dish with butter. Set aside.

PREPARE THE YUCA MASH With a fork or potato masher, mash the yuca well and mix in the butter and 1 teaspoon of salt. While it's okay if you leave a few lumps, you want to try to get the mash as smooth as you can. The mixture will seem very gelatinous. Pour in the milk and stir until all the liquid has been incorporated and the mixture begins to look like gummy mashed potatoes. Taste for seasoning and add more salt if necessary. Stir the egg yolks into the mash. Set aside.

{CONTINUED}

COOKING NOTES

INGREDIENTS

Yuca Also called cassava, manioc, or mandioca, yuca (YOO-kah) is an elongated root vegetable with a very tough and inedible brown skin and milky white flesh. It is high in starch and has a neutral flavor. It is used to make tapioca. Yuca can be purchased fresh or frozen. In the latter case, it comes peeled. If using frozen yuca in this recipe, thaw at room temperature before boiling.

TECHNIQUE

Peeling yuca Yuca has a very thick skin that is usually waxed. I find the easiest way of removing the skin is by slicing it off with a knife (rather than using a vegetable peeler). You may notice a red tinge to the flesh of the yuca that sits directly under the skin. I tend to cut that off, as it will discolor the dish. When cutting up the yuca, you may also notice some gray streaks in the flesh. These are natural and do not affect the flavor or texture of the vegetable.

ADVANCE PREPARATION

This recipe can be made a few hours in advance and left out at room temperature.

WHIP THE EGG WHITES AND FOLD THEM IN Using a handheld or stand mixer with the whisk attachment, beat the egg whites at high speed until stiff peaks form, about 4 minutes.

Using a rubber spatula, fold ¼ of the beaten egg whites into the yuca mash. Carefully fold in the remaining egg whites until just incorporated, making sure to mix gently to maintain the volume of the beaten egg whites.

BAKE THE SOUFFLÉ AND SERVE Pour the yuca mixture into the prepared baking dish and bake for 30 minutes, or until a skewer inserted in its center comes out clean. The soufflé will be puffed and lightly browned.

The soufflé will sink a bit after it is removed from the oven. Serve by slicing wedges or scooping out helpings with a large spoon.

BLACK BEAN, BACON & RICE SALAD

Feijoada (feh-shoo-AH-dah) is a typical Brazilian stew prepared with black beans and smoked pork and accompanied by white rice. This recipe takes those flavors and lightens them up, in the form of a cold rice salad. Because the salad's bright flavors are best enjoyed at room temperature, it is a great dish to serve when entertaining large crowds, as it can be made well in advance and left covered in a serving bowl. **Serves 8 to 10**

¾ pound bacon (about 18 slices), chopped
3 cups cooked white or brown rice, cooled
2 (15½-ounce cans) black beans, drained and
    rinsed
2 red bell peppers, seeded and chopped
4 green onions, trimmed, halved lengthwise and
    thinly sliced
4 plum tomatoes, cored, seeds removed,
    and diced
2 cups lightly packed cilantro leaves and tender
    stems, chopped, plus a few sprigs for garnish
Juice of 2 limes (about 3 tablespoons)
⅓ cup red wine vinegar
¼ cup extra-virgin olive oil
Salt and black pepper

FRY THE BACON Place the bacon in a dry sauté pan over medium-high heat. Sauté the bacon until it renders its fat and turns crispy and golden brown, about 8 minutes. Remove the bacon from the pan and drain on a paper towel–lined dish.

MIX THE RICE SALAD AND DRESS IT In a large bowl combine the rice, beans, red peppers, green onions, tomatoes, and cilantro and mix well.

Pour the lime juice, vinegar, and oil over the salad and toss well.

GARNISH AND SERVE Crush the bacon into small bite-size pieces and toss into the salad. Transfer the salad to a serving bowl, garnish with cilantro sprigs, and serve.

COOKING NOTES

TECHNIQUES

Cooking white rice Rice is cooked by simmering the raw grains in salted water. To make 3 cups of cooked rice, combine 1½ cups long-grain white rice, 3 cups of water, and ½ teaspoon of salt in a medium saucepan or pot, bring to a boil, cover, reduce to a simmer, and cook for 25 minutes or until the water is all absorbed and the rice is tender. (These quantities can easily be doubled or halved as needed.)

Using leftover rice Leftover plain cooked rice works very well with this recipe. Just warm the rice as instructed below in Advance Preparation and continue with the recipe.

ADVANCE PREPARATION

If you would like to make this recipe in advance, prepare the elements (bacon, rice, and bean mixture) as instructed, but do not mix them together. Store in separate airtight containers in the refrigerator. When ready to serve, warm the rice by sprinkling a little water over it and placing in the microwave for 30 seconds or heating in a pot on the stovetop. After the rice has been warmed, mix in the bean mixture and the bacon.

COCONUT CUPCAKES

In Brazil, sweet coconut confections called *cocadas* are very popular: coconut flakes are cooked in milk and sugar and formed into balls. This dessert takes the fundamental flavors and textures of that dessert and repackages them into a very light yet luscious cupcake. **Makes 24 cupcakes**

3 sticks (1½ cups) unsalted butter, at room
    temperature
2 cups sugar
4 eggs
3 cups all-purpose flour
1 tablespoon baking powder
1 teaspoon salt
1 (13½-ounce) can coconut milk
1 tablespoon vanilla extract
2 cups sweetened shredded coconut flakes

Meringue
4 egg whites
1 cup sugar
Pinch of salt

PREHEAT THE OVEN AND PREPARE THE BATTER
Preheat the oven to 325°F. Line the cups of two 12-cup cupcake pans with paper liners. Set aside.

Using a stand mixer or handheld electric mixer beat the butter and sugar together on high speed until smooth, about 2 minutes. Add the eggs and beat for another 3 minutes at high speed, until the mixture is light and fluffy, scraping the bottom of the bowl as necessary.

In a separate bowl, combine the flour, baking powder, and salt and stir well with a whisk or fork. In a new bowl, combine the coconut milk and vanilla extract and mix well. Add about ¼ of the flour mixture and ¼ of the coconut milk mixture to the butter and egg mixture and beat on medium speed until combined. Continue adding the flour mixture and the coconut milk mixture in batches until all the ingredients are combined. Turn the mixer off and, using a wooden spoon or rubber spatula, gently fold in 1 cup of the shredded coconut flakes.

BAKE THE CUPCAKES Transfer the cake batter to a liquid measuring cup for easy pouring and fill the cupcake liners ¾ of the way full. Bake the cupcakes for 30 minutes, or until a toothpick or skewer inserted in the center of a cake comes out clean. Note that the tops will be a bit pale.

Allow the cupcakes to cool in the pan for 15 minutes. Transfer the cupcakes to a cooling rack and allow to cool for another 15 minutes.

TOAST THE COCONUT While the cupcakes are cooling, spread the remaining cup of coconut flakes in a single layer on a baking sheet. Toast in the 325°F oven for 7 minutes, stir the flakes a bit, and toast for another 5 minutes, or until most of the flakes are golden brown. Stay close to the oven during the last 5 minutes, as the flakes can quickly burn. Remove from the oven and set aside.

PREPARE THE MERINGUE Place the egg whites, sugar, and salt in the work bowl of a stand mixer or a metal mixing bowl and set it over a pot of simmering water. Stir until the sugar is dissolved and the egg whites are warm to the touch, about 4 minutes. The mixture will be a bit frothy and milky in color.

Remove the bowl from the pot and beat on high speed until the egg whites are stiff and glossy, about 5 minutes. (If you are using a stand mixer, beat with the whisk attachment.)

ASSEMBLE THE CUPCAKES Spread the meringue over the cupcakes and garnish each with a sprinkling of the toasted coconut flakes.

Elote a la parilla, 33–35

Empanadas
    Beef Empanadas, 143–46
    commercial dough for, 146
    Sausage and Mushroom
        Empanadas, 143–46

Endive, Green Onions and
    Tomatoes, Grilled, 137

Ensalada de aguacate, 87

Espresso. *See* Coffee

F

Fish
    Chile-Rubbed Tuna Steak with
        Avocado and Lime, 46
    Fresh Fish Ceviche with Ginger
        and Chile, 107–8
    Grilled Mahi-mahi with Mango
        Salsa, 81
    grilling, 81
    Wood Plank–Grilled Halibut, 162

Flan, Dulce de Leche, 138–39

Flare-ups, 9, 133

Flavor injectors, 84

Fletán a la parrilla, 162

Frita cubana, 75–76

Frostings and icings
    Cajeta Buttercream, 38–39
    Lime Icing, 88–89

Fuente de camarones al ajillo,
    77–78

G

Gallo pinto, 65

Garlic
    Arugula-, Garlic-, and Green
        Onion–Stuffed Flank Steak,
        147–48
    Brown Sugar–Crusted Grilled
        Chicken, 98–99
    Chilean Hot Pepper Salsa, 166
    Citrus Garlic Marinade, 82, 83
    Fresh Parsley Sauce, 152
    Mojo, 77
    paste, 152

Gas, grilling with, 11

Glazes, 15
    using, 15

Grates, oiling, 9

Green onions, 31
    Arugula-, Garlic-, and Green
        Onion–Stuffed Flank Steak,
        147–48

Charred Green Onions, 31
Grilled Endive, Green Onions and
    Tomatoes, 137

Grilling
    with charcoal, 12–14
    with gas, 11
    tips, 8–10
    with wood, 11–12

Grill toppers, 94

Guacamole
    Chipotle Guacamole, 22–23
    Traditional Guacamole, 22

Guava
    Guava Ketchup, 75–76
    juice, 58
    Rum and Guava Cooler, 58

H

Habanero chiles, 53
    Fiery Tomato Salsa, 53
    Spicy Yellow Chile Sauce, 116

Halibut, 162
    Fresh Fish Ceviche with Ginger
        and Chile, 107–8
    Wood Plank–Grilled Halibut, 162

Ham
    Grilled Cuban Sandwich, 90–91
    Medianoche Sandwich, 90

Honey
    Honey–Apple Cider Vinegar
        Glaze, 50
    Honey-Lime Glaze, 27

Huancaina Sauce, 119

Humita de olla, 154

I

Icings. *See* Frostings and icings

J

Jalapeño chiles, 37
    Beer-Stewed Beans with Chiles,
        37–38
    Fiery Tomato Salsa, 53
    Grilled Quesadillas with Charred
        Poblano and Jalapeño Chiles,
        19–21
    Lime-Marinated Shrimp and Crab
        Cocktail, 44–45
    Mango Salsa, 81

Jicama, 54
    Crunchy Jicama and Lime
        Salad, 54
    peeling and cutting, 54

L

Leche de tigre, 108

Lechon asado, 82–84

Lemons
    Grilled Endive, Green Onions and
        Tomatoes, 137
    grilling, 137, 153

Lettuce
    Grilled Salad, 172–73
    Mixed Green Salad, 66
    Salad of Marinated Cheese, Olives
        and Tomatoes, 168
    tearing, 66

Limes
    Caipiroska, 172
    Chile-Rubbed Tuna Steak with
        Avocado and Lime, 46
    Citrus and Oregano Marinade,
        29–30
    Citrus Garlic Marinade, 82, 83
    Coconut-Lime Glaze, 175
    Crunchy Jicama and Lime
        Salad, 54
    Fiery Tomato Salsa, 53
    Fresh Fish Ceviche with Ginger
        and Chile, 107–8
    Frozen Limeade Margarita, 18
    Grilled Corn and Quinoa Salad,
        121–22
    Hot Pepper and Lime Sauce, 180
    Lime Icing, 88–89
    Lime-Marinated Shrimp and Crab
        Cocktail, 44–45
    Mango Salsa, 81
    Margarita, 18
    Mojito, 72
    Mojo, 77
    Mushroom Ceviche, 108
    Shrimp Ceviche, 109

Lomo al trapo, 95–96

M

Maduros a la parrilla con crema, 59

*Mahi a la parrilla con salsa de
    mango,* 81

Mahi-mahi, 81
    Fresh Fish Ceviche with Ginger
        and Chile, 107–8
    Grilled Mahi-mahi with Mango
        Salsa, 81

Malagueta peppers, 180
    Hot Pepper and Lime Sauce, 180

To Gerard and his appetite

Published in the United States by Ten Speed Press, an imprint of the
Crown Publishing Group, a division of Random House, Inc., New York.
www.crownpublishing.com
www.tenspeed.com

Ten Speed Press and the Ten Speed Press colophon are registered
trademarks of Random House, Inc.

Library of Congress Cataloging-in-Publication Data
Castro, Lourdes, 1971 Dec. 9–
    Latin grilling : recipes to share, from Argentine asado to Yucatecan
barbecue and more / Lourdes Castro.
        p. cm.
    Includes index.
    Summary: "Respected Latin chef and cooking teacher Lourdes Castro
takes readers on a culinary tour of the Americas, firing up 90 recipes
arranged into ten grilling fiestas that feature authentic Latin American
flavors, all tailored for the home cook or backyard griller." —Provided by
publisher.
    ISBN 978-1-60774-004-9 (pbk.)
    1. Barbecuing—Latin America. 2. Cooking, Latin American. 3. Cook-
books. I. Title.
    TX840.B3C45 2011
    641.598—dc22

                                    2010048745

ISBN 978-1-60774-004-9

Printed in China

Design by Katy Brown
Food styling by Lourdes Castro
Prop styling by Martha Bernabe

10 9 8 7 6 5 4 3 2 1

First Edition